Stop Acting Your Age, Start Living Your Life

from the creator of ZOOMER© ... Boomers with Zip!

Dr. David James Demko PhD

Clinical Gerontologist, and
Certified Retirement Planner

Founder and Editor
AgeVenture News Service and ZOOMER Magazine

ISBN-13: 978-1453802465

ISBN-10: 1453802460

LCCN: 2010913361

CreateSpace, North Charleston, SC

Dedication

Sharon, Rachel, Maura, Peyton, Ryker, Chris Stringer, Nick Stallard

Contents

Acknowledgements

To Zig Ziglar and John C. Maxwell, authors of *The 21 Irrefutable Laws of Leadership* (1998), the textbook used to teach my Leadership Seminar at Miami Dade Honors College that same year. The authors inspired me to create a list of irrefutable traits describing a Boomer Innovator called ZOOMER (a boomer with Zip). Despite their chronological age, Zoomers pursue *youthful* maturity, a lifestyle that's decades younger than their boomer peers.

To the Center for Science in the Public Interest (www.cspinet. org) which monitors the efficacy of research reports, helping consumers understand the difference between scientific knowledge and pop culture hyperbole.

To the National Institutes of Health (www.nih.gov) for providing the trustworthy, cutting-edge research identifying the multi-disciplinary essentials for living a healthy, active and productive lifestyle.

To the Boomers who's *AgeVenturous* lifestyles portray the ZOOMER spirit; first reported in the inaugural issue of *ZOOMER magazine*, April 1998, and now recounted here to inspire a new vision for ultra-modern style of maturity.

To the emerging Zoomer Nation, an extraordinary subculture within the Boomer demographic who are re-inventing modern maturity; coloring outside the lines, zigzagging and zooming toward a bright new horizon chock-full of possibilities, redefining the meaning of maturity and retirement in the new millennium.

1

Youth'n Up Your Life

The human body is built to last 120 years, but life expectancy is only 80 years. You can get back those lost 40 years.

In 1974, I discovered a book, "Nobody Ever Died of Old Age" authored by Sharon Curtin, a nurse who wrote about her aging father. The author recalled how her Dad was, again and again, diagnosed with a life-threatening malady and given a short time to live. However, the old man managed to cheat death each time. What doesn't kill us makes us stronger. Years later, he did meet his Maker. As I recall, he was hit by a truck while walking home from a Saturday night dance.

The moral of the story? If you want to change your life, then change the way you live it. Everyone wants to live a long time, but nobody wants to grow old. Sounds like a contradiction in terms. It's not. Living longer and staying younger, as this book will demonstrate, are compatible goals.

First of all, our generation's pursuit of a longer, healthier, active life is totally backwards. There is too much emphasis on "stopping our aging process" and "too little emphasis on preserving our youth." What is the purpose of living 100 years, unless those extra years are lived with vim and vigor?

Sure, we can't stop accumulating birthdays, but we can *Youth'n Up* each passing year. So, "Stop acting your age and start living your life."

Youth'n Up" your life is a philosophy for both successful aging (adding years to your life) and successful youthing (adding life to those years). Time to learn from boomers who are the same chronological age as you, yet living a more youthful, energetic, optimistic, and passionate lifestyle. This is your opportunity to join the emerging Zoomer Nation?

Let's get started with a very significant fact that can change your life. Did you know that 80 percent of longevity (how long you will live) is determined by lifestyle factors, not the aging process? In other words, our youth is eroded due to a lifestyle of self-neglect. The scientific evidence in support of this new reality continues to mount as reported by the National Geographic Society's global research on longevity trends. "The average American could live an extra 12 years and be 40% happier by optimizing their lifestyle and environment," (The Blue Zones, 2010).

The human body is built to last 120 years. That's the number of years scientists call the maximum potential human *life span*. However, our average *life-expectancy* is 80 years. Time to find out where those missing 40 years have gone, and how to get them back.

Welcome to Zoomer Nation

There's a totally new kind of boomer, the kind who stands out from the crowd. These new boomers are coloring outside the lines, zigzagging and zooming toward a bright new horizon chock-full of possibilities for reinventing retirement and redefining what it means to be a mature adult in the new millennium.

Are you a Boomer?

You are if your birthday falls between 1946 and 1964. That birth period defines you as a member of the baby boom generation. However, birth dates alone don't tell you much about how a person thinks or acts. Not all boomers think and act the same. Some are boomer zoomers who are breaking new ground, re-defining aging, and re-inventing retirement. Zoomer is a term coined (Demko, 1998) to brand this trend-setting subculture within the boomer generation known as Zoomer Nation.

Are you a Zoomer?

The answer is "yes," if you've have managed to acquire the following nine Zoomer traits. Each trait's description includes an example of the many web sites where you can get expert information on how to acquire that Zoomer trait. The more traits acquired, the better your chances of living a longer, healthier and active life. Food Fitness is the first trait.

Food Fitness: eat your way to better health

Zoomers adhere to a nutritional and caloric dietary plan based on functional age, gender, BMI and level of activity.

Food Facts - Get started at: www.usda.gov

Supplement Facts - Start at: nccam.nih.gov/health/supplements

Brain Fitness: boomer brain boosters

Zoomers perform daily brain exercises to sustain memory, learning, and problem-solving skills. Cultivates a keen sense of intellectual curiosity that fosters continued cognitive growth.

Get started at: www.www.nlm.nih.gov/medlineplus/memory.html

Physical Fitness: exercise, energize, revitalize

Zoomer fitness regimens combine both aerobics (for energy and endurance) and anaerobics (for strength and flexibility).

Get started at: www.nia.nih.gov/exercise

Social Fitness: grow your social network

Zoomers orchestrate a social support system of companions, close friends, and a confidante. Outgoing, good listener, empathetic.

Get started at: www.aarp.org/personal-growth

Identity Fitness: re-invent yourself

Zoomers enjoy a positive self-concept, self-effacing sense of humor, and a passion for living life to the fullest.
Get started at: www.encore.org/learn/aboutprograms

Spiritual Fitness: connect with a higher power

Zoomers create a broad repertoire of coping skills that incorporate the undeniable strengths of science and faith.
Get started at: www.PurposeDrivenLife.com

Retirement Readiness

Zoomers engage in early, sound (financial, health, lifestyle) retirement planning capable of supporting their anticipated standard of living. The Certified Financial Planner (CFP) is an authoritative credential to look for in the selection of a retirement planning advisor.
Get started at AARP's financial web.
www.aarp.org/money

Intellectual Fitness: Get Age-Smart

Zoomers know the difference between primary (inevitable) and secondary (reversible) aging. They monitor health risks in order to reduce morbidity and mortality risk factors, adding years to their life and life to their years.
Get started at the University of Wisconsin Healthy Aging Center.
www.ssc.wisc.edu/cdha/data/dataresources.html

Constantly Curious: Stay Age Smart

A Zoomer cultivates a keen sense of intellectual curiosity, relying on trusted sources of healthy aging research.
Get started at the National Archive of Computerized Data on Aging.
http://www.icpsr.umich.edu/icpsrweb/NACDA/studies/4690

Zoomers are boomers with zip!

Zoomers serve as inspirational role-models for age-peers and future retirees through active participation in society such as engaging in second careers, voluntary service, advocacy, performing arts, and elective office.

Get started with certified Zoomer Profiles.

www.ZoomerBoomerMagazine.com

The new Zoomer Nation is far removed from traditional stereotypes that portray senior adults as passive, frail, and broke. Members of Zoomer Nation will live a longer, healthier, and more prosperous retirement than any time in history (U.S. Census).

Retirement Re-invented

Back in 1900, workers spent an average of 14 months in retirement, because no one stopped working unless they became disabled or seriously ill. Life expectancy in 1900 was only 49 years. Today, those who retire at age 65 can expect to live at least another 15 years. More years, better health and financial preparation have given boomers great expectations for their retirement years which has spawned an enormous retirement living industry of products and services promising to fulfill every boomer expectation.

Words of caution on retirement—start planning early. Your longer, more active retirement years will require substantial financing in order to continue the standard of living to which you have become accustomed. Conventional wisdom is you will need 80% of your work income to sustain your current lifestyle in retirement, plus a hedge against inflation.

Life in the ZOOMER Lane

One in ten boomers is expected to live at least one hundred years according to the U.S. Census Bureau. In contrast, the odds for Zoomers are projected to be 300 percent higher, three in ten will live at least 100 years (AgeVenture News, Zoomer-boomer longitudinal study, 1998-2008). Zoomers gain a longevity-edge because their healthy lifestyle traits are specifically designed to lower a multitude of risk factors.

The following chapter introduces 13 Zoomers from among a total of 144 profiled in Zoomer magazine since the inaugural issue in 1998.

Read their inspirational stories, then start your own AgeVenturous journey from boomer to Zoomer and beyond.

ZOOMER-FRIENDLY READING – LONGEVITY

How to Live to Be 100 (and not regret it) – TIME magazine
www.time.com/time/magazine/article/0,9171,994967,00.html

Secrets of the Wellderly - Wall Street Journal
www.wsj.com/article/SB122176857706253591.html

Secrets of Living Longer : The Blue Zones – National Geographic, 2010aphic.com/ngm/0511/sights_n_sounds/index.html

Is 100 the new 80? – Scientific American
www.scientificamerican.com/longevity

Selling the Fountain of Youth: how the anti-aging industry made a disease out of getting old
Weintraub (2010).

The Right Questions: for an Extraordinary Life
Ford (2004).

It's Never Too Late to Plant a Tree: 65 Inspiring Stories
Helitzer and Helitzer (2003).

Life Gets Better: the unexpected pleasures of growing older
Lustbader (2011).

The Art of Growing Old: aging with grace
Hennezel (2012).

Nobody Ever Died of Old Age
Curtin (1974).

2

Zoomers ... Boomers With Zip!

Zoomers serve as inspirational role-models for age-peers and future retirees through active participation in society.

An elder of the village was asked, "Have you lived here all your life?' The elder answered, "Not yet." Here's the point. Do you consider yourself a "finished product" or a "work in progress?" Is your life over, or do you still have "miles and miles to go before you sleep" (Robert Frost)?

Chances are some of your hopes and dreams have remained dormant all these years because you had to focus all your energy on career preparation, landing the right job, climbing the career ladder, building a strong marriage, raising children and getting them ready to launch lives of their own.

Time flew by, and now you're sitting there in your empty nest wondering what's in store for the rest of your life. You're free from past responsibilities, but free to do what? . The answer to that question congers up an image of the "other you" that's been dormant all these years. The "you" just waiting to come out. Perhaps, there is an artist, explorer, or novelist just waiting to emerge. Take your cue from AARP's slogan, "What do you want to be when you grow-up?"

Who are your heroes, your sources of inspiration? Just thinking about them brings a smile to your face. What's the attraction? It's how they enrich your life with a sense of joy, childlike wonder and limitless possibilities in life. Your heroes have traits you hoped to incorporate into your persona. Now it's your turn to spread your wings and fly. There are examples to follow.

Zoomers are boomers with Zip! The phrase refers to boomers who appear decades younger than others who are the same chronological age. Their *youthful* maturity isn't defined by physical appearance alone. Instead, they appear youthful because they think and behave that way. Energetic, intellectually curious, adventurous. Still setting and achieving personal growth goals.

A youthful maturity is yours for the taking. Today's 50-plus adult is better educated, healthier, more affluent and forward-looking than any previous generation. What's more, life-expectancy is thirty years longer today. In 1900, life-expectancy was 49 years. Today's life-expectancy is 80 years.

What are you waiting for? Time to release the "other you" that's being dormant and can now be realized.

The following profiles are not of super-rich, globe-trotting celebrities whose active lifestyles are made possible by an entourage of personal trainers, private chefs, and personal assistants. The people featured here are just like you who have been featured over the years since 1998 in my syndicated feature column, ZOOMER (AgeVenture Syndicated News Service which focuses on ordinary people pursuing extraordinary lives.

The following Zoomers are my personal favorites. Their stories of courage, innovation, and hope have been a continuing source of inspiration. It is my sincere hope that these remarkable individuals will open windows of infinite possibilities for you. Names of the Zoomers are listed, below, in the order in which they appear in the following pages.

➤ Michael Flynt, ZOOMER™ August 2007
➤ Tackling college Football at age 59.
➤ Anne Dimon, ZOOMER™ October 2010
➤ Her office is a sun-swept beach.
➤ Jane and Brent Cassie, ZOOMER™ July 2010
➤ Second careers as photo-journalists.
➤ Radha Sahar, ZOOMER™ November 2010
➤ Composer-performer of Boomer Rock.
➤ Kathy Keefe & Kim Renton, ZOOMER™ May 2010
➤ "Hockey moms" invent EnVy pillow.
➤ Pat Boswell, ZOOMER™ February 2010
➤ Environment-friendly entrepreneur.
➤ Sue Mead, ZOOMER™ September 2011
➤ Celebrates 60th birthday during 16-day auto race.
➤ Kristin Kutac Ward, ZOOMER™ December 2010
➤ Assessing retirement housing options via computer.
➤ Barbara Waxman, ZOOMER™ January 2011
➤ Blazing pro-retirement trails for Boomers.
➤ Suzanne Andrews, ZOOMER™ March 2010
➤ Functional fitness made fun.
➤ Jeri Maier, ZOOMER™ October 1998
➤ The boomers are coming, the boomers are coming !
➤ Rita Golden Gelman, ZOOMER™ February 2002
➤ Globe-trotting author rejoices, Email changed my life !
➤ Marshall Ulrich, ZOOMER™ May 2012
➤ From sea to shining sea, boomer runs across USA.

Get inspired. Who knows, your story just might appear in a future issue of ZOOMER magazine, or the next edition of this book. Email your story to: ZoomerNation@demko.com

Photo Top: Number 49 celebrates.
Bottom: private moment (L), on the field (C), headshot (R).

Michael Flynt, ZOOMER™ August 2007

"It ain't over 'til it's over" said sport's great Yogi Berra. Fifty-nine-year-old baby boomer, Michael Flynt has taken that advice to heart... and right back into the football stadium as a varsity player for Sul Ross State University (SRSU). "It's true, he (Flynt) made the team," says SRSU's Saul Garza, executive director of alumni relations at SRSU's campus in Alpine, Texas.

Alpine is a town of 6,000 residents. But that all changed, as dozens of news agencies ascended onto SRSU's campus to interview the new student-athlete who is the "World's Oldest College Football Player."

"It all started," says Garza, "during a Baby Boomers (class of 1965-1974) reunion of 200 alumnae convened in San Antonio." The boomers got to talking about their college years, which prompted Flynt contemplate his return to college and finish his degree.

His motivation to return to football occurred while he was drinking beer and swapping stories with some old football buddies. He brought up the biggest regret of his life: Getting kicked off the college team before his senior year.

An exploratory phone call to SRS led to Flynt's discovery that he was still eligible to return to campus and finish his degree. Flynt was living in Franklin, Tennessee at the time of the phone call. After he told his wife about his dream to return to school, they put their home up for sale and relocated to Alpine, Texas, near the Big Bend National Park, a three-hour drive from the nearest airport.

Now back on campus, Flynt asked his old football coach about the prospect of "getting back in the game." After a brief exchange of "you've got to be kidding," Flynt heard the coach say, "You still have one more season of eligibility." It was history in the making!

READ MORE: www.mikeflynt.com
Photo Credit: Sul Ross State Univ and Michael Flynt, USA.

Photo Top: rock-climbing respite (L), marathon runner (R).
Photo Bottom: backpacking (L), retail therapy (R).

Anne Dimon, ZOOMER™ October 2010

Ask Anne Dimon about her ZOOMER credentials, and you will get the following answer. "I'm a Zoomer who has climbed Mt. Kenya, trekked to the bottom of the Grand Canyon, crawled through the Cuchi Tunnels of Vietnam, swam with stingray, and took up running in my early 50s."

A travel writer/columnist/editor for more than two decades, Anne is the CEO of www.TravelToWellness.com. Anne's website, features the world's best health spa resorts. This energetic entrepreneur set out on a nine-day, six-airline excursion to Toronto – London - Hong Kong - Bangkok - Singapore - Johannesburg - New York - Frankfurt - Toronto to research a story on the Best Beds in Business Class. "Yup," says Anne, "nine days."

However, all work and no play can get really borrrrrrrrrrrring!!! So, what's a girl to do? Anne's remedy? "Retail Therapy"...also known as "Shop 'til you drop." During Anne's "off road" travel time, you are likely to find her waist deep in a virtual sea of bargains. One of her favorite "shop spots" is Dubai where (photo) she is surrounded by a mountain of native-made fabric of all kinds.

It's often said that man's best friend is a dog. But a ZOOMER's best friend is what allows you to become a rover. According to Anne, "Give me my laptop, Blackberry, and Wi-Fi, and I can work from anywhere in the world. Sometimes," says the world traveler, "I'm hard at work on the rocky shores of a sun-swept Jamaican beach.

"It may not sound like work to you, but it's a ZOOMER thing I guess, and it works for me."

Check out what ZOOMER, Anne Dimon has achieved. Her story will inspire you to pursue the new directions, challenges, and opportunities that lay ahead in your future.

READ MORE: www.traveltowellness.com
Photo Credit: Anne Dimon, Canada.

Jane and Brent Cassie

Photo Top: on the slopes.

Photo Bottom: marketing (L), snow sledding (R).

Jane and Brent Cassie, ZOOMER™ July 2010

Jane Cassie's dogsled "heads for the hills" (photo, bottom right) in Canada's British Columbia. Jane is a travel writer, and husband, Brent is a photo journalist who captures every moment of their travel adventures. These ZOOMERs are rising stars in the Canadian travel industry. For them, retirement is a New Beginning. "We both plan to retire this year in June to explore the world together," says Jane, a bright smile beaming from her face. "Brent will retire from his teaching position, and I'll leave nursing to expand my travel writing portfolio."

"It's been an evolutionary process." Home and work are in Surrey, British Columbia. But more and more these days, the energetic couple retreat to the majestic solitude of their vacation home at Big Bear Lake. "It's a great opportunity to reconnect with nature, reflect on life, and write." The couple first met at age seventeen back in 1970 and dated for two years, but life sent each along different paths. Twenty-three years later, they reunited and married in 1994.

The couple shares a youthful enthusiasm for life and a robust hope for whatever the future has in store. Perhaps all that positive, hopeful energy is due to their work with children. Jane's spent the last two decades at Fraser Health Authority as a nursing coordinator for Nursing Support Services, a program that targets children with special needs. Brent is an elementary school teacher, helping the little ones prepare for their journey into that great big world out there.

"For the past fourteen years I've been a part-time freelance travel writer, and Brent has been my travel companion, part-time photographer, and editor," says Jane. With their retirement clock ticking away, these travel writers have a busy schedule of projects and press trips. "We currently have 17 contributing writers and every 6 months produce a CD of 26 fresh travel stories and accompanying images for our editors."

READ MORE: www.travelwriterstales.com
Photo Credit: Jane and Brent Cassie, Canada.

Radha Sahar

Photo Top: composing Boomer Rock.
Photo Middle Row: playing guitar (L), with the boys in the band (R).
Photo Bottom Row: meal prep (L), yoga time (R).

Radha Sahar, ZOOMER™ November 2010

Radha Sahar is a musician, composer, and producer of ballads about "all things boomer." She describes her songs as "rebellious, touching and humorous rock/pop songs," a.k.a. BOOMER ROCK. Her band, Baby Boomer Girl, "emerged in a burst of writing inspired by the joy of having a lovely new man in my life," says Radha.

Her Web site bio is formatted in the fun rock-music tradition of sex, drugs, and Rock-n-roll. Here's her take on all three, a bit more toned down with the passage of time.

SEX: "My music pulses with born-again enthusiasm for the joys of love. I've been through the mill with broken marriages, and now in a new-love relationship (met him on the internet)."

DRUGS: Drugs now mean things like "vitamin pills, progesterone, and detox cleansing herbal sweep from the local health shop."

ROCK-N-ROLL: The songs her band performs "touch my heart with high-energy rock played with a dose of light relief."

It's not all fun and games. Radha is dead serious about healthy living. She follows exercise regimes, gets deep sleep, walks, swims, and practices yoga. Her goal for her "second season" of life is to avoid being "a medicated old codger, a boring old fart, or a grumpy old cynic." She says, at her age "who cares what party-poopers think?"

Her signature song and her band have the same name, "Baby Boomer Girl." Her latest album is out on the "Won't Sit Down" recording label.

"It's time for this grandmother of three to strut on stage, fire-up boomers everywhere to live it up, and hit #1 on the music charts."

"Let's rock, sing & dance while we still can" (Radha Sahar).

READ MORE: babyboomergirl.wordpress.com
Photo Credit: Boomer Girl, New Zealand.

Kathy Keefe

Kim Renton

Hockey Moms Invent Anti-aging Pillow

The next generation of pillow

Photo Top: Kathy and Kim face-off on the ice.
Photo Bottom: enviable bedroom packed with the power-pillow.

Kathy Keefe & Kim Renton, ZOOMER™ May 2010

"Pillow Angst" is the quest for the perfect pillow. A common predicament shared by sleepless boomers, until they become restful clients who now sleep on an "EnVy Pillow," created by hockey-mom-entrepreneurs, Kathy and Kim.

Rest assured, their invention has become a global sensation. EnVy Pillow® is now patented in Europe, Canada and the USA. Kathy, says, the quest for the perfect pillow started in her 30's, when she began to feel sleepless effects of corrective back surgery for scoliosis.

"Waking up with pain, ice packs and Advil became my morning routine," recalls Kathy, a Registered Intensive Care Nurse. "The quest for the right pillow became an obsession!"

"Apparently there was an upside to my sleep pattern, no sleep lines. My hockey buddy, Kim made the connection and it was the start of a business partnership." According to Kathy, "Kim is the co-creator of EnVy and, quite honestly, the "brains" behind our business venture." Kim is a Critical Care Nurse Administrator and Botox Medical Consultant. As co-founder of our company, Kim found that "sleep lines" associated with insomnia were a reversible condition, thanks to restful sleep, courtesy of the EnVy pillow.

Running into each other was truly karma. Figuratively and factually. "I recall our initial meeting was during a match between Hockey Mom teams. Within a short time, we created a design for an anti-aging pillow, ergonomically designed to create sound sleep and reduce the risk of facial wrinkles.

The duo's company received accolades from plastic surgeons, sleep specialists, dermatologists, chiropractors, physiotherapists and satisfied customers on three continents.

"Hockey-moms RULE !!!"

READ MORE: www.envypillow.com
Photo Credit: Kathy Keefe and Kim Renton, Canada.

Photo Top: the entrepreneur.
Photo Bottom: Pat's invention (L), product-testing (R).

Pat Boswell, ZOOMER™ February 2010

"Go Green" has become the new mantra for our environmentally conscious society and thankfully, nearly everyone who is anyone has jumped on the bandwagon. However, there were many forward thinking business-minds who were already on-board before the Green train left the station. Meet Patricia Boswell.

Pat Boswell is the creator of Safonique, an all-natural, hypoallergenic and powerful laundry detergent that's in tune with the needs of consumers and the environment. She is also founder and CEO of Browell Industries, Inc, the company that produces her award-winning product.

Boswell first conceived of an all-natural detergent in the early 1990s. Her original mission was to target the baby market with a powdered detergent. She concocted the early versions of it with essential oils in her home kitchen. It took over a decade to fine-tune the product, which evolved into the Safonique of today – a pure aromatherapy, environmentally sensitive liquid detergent for the entire family.

Boswell first entered the professional world as a nurse, but soon stepped beyond the healthcare field into business, earning a BA and MBA in business that complemented her real estate license and certification in financial planning

The evolution of Safonique took place even as she kept busy as the mother of a son who is attending college and a daughter who is a busy pre-teen, and as the wife of a college basketball coach. In 2006, Pat co-founded "Teaming 4 Life," a non-profit organization created by three coaches wives dedicated to increasing the awareness of cancer detection and prevention. When not building her business, Boswell fines time to give-back to her community, providing training for aspiring entrepreneurs.

READ MORE: www.safonique.com
Photo Credit: Safonique, USA.

Sue Mead, 1st woman to win 5,903-mile auto race

Photo Top: prep for all those miles and miles yet to go.
Photo Bottom: miles and miles of winning smiles.

Sue Mead, ZOOMER™ September 2011

Sue Mead is an automotive and adventure journalist with very impressive "stats" as an auto racer. Her career spans decades of test-driving, intensive road-trips and racing four-wheel-drive vehicles in locations around the globe.

Fulfilling a lifelong dream to compete in the most famous rally on the planet, Mead celebrated her 60th birthday behind the wheel of the Ford Raptor driving a daunting 5,903-mile race called the Dakar Rally. That race-adventure took sixteen grueling days, from Buenos Aires to the Atacama Desert in Chile.

"The Dakar was brutal," said Mead. "The majority (two-thirds) of the contestants failed to complete the race." Sue's race team was the only U.S. contestant to finish. "We took home the trophy."

Sue is the first woman auto driver from either North or South America to compete in Dakar's auto race. Her track record includes:

- The Arctic Circle Challenge '95, the Tip to Tip Challenge '96,
- Transamerica Challenge '97,
- The 1996, 1999, 2000, 2002, and 2003 Baja 1000.
- Paris-Dakar-Cairo 2000 .
- SCORE 1999 Primm 300.

In 2008, Sue's off-road racing achievements earned her induction into the Off-Road Motorsports Hall of Fame. Her exploits are also featured in a race film documentary, "Into the Dust."

In typical Zoomer-fashion, this globe-trotting, off-road racing champion still finds windows of opportunity for giving back to her community. "I have been blessed to travel to 69 countries and perform goodwill projects in South America, Haiti, and New Orleans with Katrina victims."

This ZOOMER runs on auto-pilot.

See more at: www.youtube.com/watch?v=lmH2cPQc0AI
Photo Credit: Sue Mead, USA.

Photo: using the Retiring by Design program.

Kristin Kutac Ward, ZOOMER™ December 2010

It's a sign of our times. Kristin's web site, RetiringbyDesign.com offers boomers expert help, exploring retirement living and housing options. Her web brands itself as a comprehensive and fun way to search for the retirement community that fits you like a glove.

The web site's network of twenty thousand retirement communities is continually updated with photos and documents submitted by retirement communities operating in all fifty states.

Kristin's planning process begins with a client "self-assessment quiz" used to create a highly personalized profile of retirement needs and desires. The result of this assessment and analysis of retirement living preferences is a comprehensive plan to help zero-in on the best fit between your preferences and a fifty-state network of retirement living communities, each with a distinct culture and set of amenities.

Ward and her team crafted the Web portal after hearing firsthand the frustrations expressed by retirees and their families. "Time and again, retirees told us their biggest obstacle was not finding information on retirement communities.

What retirees need is a decision-making strategy for selecting the right community to fit their needs. RetiringbyDesign is designed to solve that problem and make the process fun," says Ward.

1st. Visitors complete a "retirement preference" quiz.
2nd Quiz results generate a holistic profile of needs.
3rd A profile of needs is matched with senior living options.
4th A Match Meter evaluates the choice of options.
5th Quiz-taker reviews "need to know" articles.
6th Quiz-taker re-thinks options, finding a better senior living fit.

It's the end of Cookie Cutter marketing to the new retiree.

READ MORE: www.retiringbydesign.com
Photo Credit: Kristin Kutac Ward, USA.

Barbara Waxman

How to Love Your Retirement
The Guide to the Best of Your Life

- Staying Healthy and Fit
- Keeping Your Mind and Spirit Young
- Doing Good, Volunteering and Making a Difference
- Planning for Financial Independence — Even if You're Starting Late
- Traveling and Relocating
- Making Friends and Keeping Romance in Your Life

AMERICA'S #1
RETIREMENT
ADVICE GUIDE
by Hundreds of
Retirees, Planners
and Consultants

Photo Top: Waxman scouting the range of mid-life opportunities.
Photo Bottom: Her new book, How to Love Your Retirement."

Barbara Waxman, ZOOMER™ January 2011

There's a new marshal in Retirement Town who's rounding up boomers, helping them head for the hills of prosperity. A bit of a maverick, Waxman is blazing new trails for Boomers.

Barbara's mission is to reframe retirement as an opportunity to begin a new and exciting phase of life. She communicates this theme in her workshops and one-on-one coaching sessions with clients.

"Boomers will approach this stage of life with the same zeal as they did in their youth." So, whatever notions you have about maturity and retirement, well, that was then, and this is now. Barbara has rebranded modern maturity as "pro-retirement," the most rewarding and productive years of our lives.

However, redefining a life stage comes with anxieties and challenges:

- Getting retirement-ready
- Coping with 24/7 spousal lifestyle
- Pondering the relocation question
- Discovering new passions
- Embracing healthy total fitness

Barbara believes the best way to answer questions for those on the cusp of retirement is to analyze the thoughts and wisdom of people who have successfully planned, and now live, their retirement dream.

Barbara Waxman serves as president of the Odyssey Group, an executive and life coaching company for mid-life adults. She founded Odyssey in 2005 in order to support age forty-plus adults to maximize their capacity to succeed at home and at work, and of course, as they explore the frontier of retirement.

Barbara considers herself a lifelong student, and she loves hiking, cooking, yoga, and stepping just outside of her comfort zone.

Read more at: www.theodysseygroup.net
Photo Credit: Barbara Waxman, USA.

Photo: Suzanne on the cover of her Functional Fitness DVD.

Suzanne Andrews, ZOOMER™ March 2010

The senior living industry has expanded to such proportions that it's become an exercise in ... EXERCISE. 78 million baby boomers, plus 30 million current retirees are causing the fitness industry to grow at a fever pitch.

That's good news to Suzanne Andrews. For the past 30 years, she's managed to put FUN into Fitness. Suzanne is a licensed occupational therapist. What better credentials for putting more Zip into the boomer lifestyle?

Unlike other fitness programs that call for tons of new exercise equipment, Suzanne's program offers an at-home workout using, of all things, household products, like cans of soup, as weight-lifting tools. Suzanne calls her program, Functional Fitness because the focus is on strengthening the body mechanics you use every day.

To date, this prolific entrepreneur has produced eight 30-minute DVDs on functional fitness targeting:

- Diabetes: improve circulation
- Brain Power: memory boosters
- Fat Burning: plus-size shape ups
- Pain Free: back and neck
- COPD and Asthma: breathe easier
- Bone Builder: fit osteoporosis
- Better Balance: decrease fall risks

Suzanne's latest FUNCTIONAL FITNESS DVD targets arthritis and helps reduce pain, stiffness, and improve flexibility so you can keep up with your grand kids.

Suzanne is now the star of a new PBS TV show on WDSC TV 15 at Dayton State College Public Broadcasting.

READ MORE: www.HealthWiseExercise.com
Photo Credit: Suzanne Andrews, USA.

Photo Top: Boomer International web site logo
Photo Bottom: Maier in the 60's (L) and today (R).

Jeri Maier, ZOOMER™ October 1998

"The boomers are coming. The boomers are coming. Millions and millions of boomers. Like a modern-day Paul Revere, entrepreneur Jeri Maier is helping America get ready for the baby boomers that are impacting every sector of society. Maier has created a place in cyberspace, Boomers International (www.boomersint.org) is the first-ever Social Network created exclusively for the boomer generation.

Name a product or service industry, and chances are it's being adapted to meet the needs of the boomers. What's on their minds these days? What are they likely to do next? These questions are being answered by gerontrepreneur, Jeri Maier. Gerontrepreneurs are business people who create industries to serve Aging America.

What prompted Jeri to start the Boomers website? "While attending college part time, working full time and with family needing attention; I used the Internet to visit many university websites to search for references for my research. It was great. I never had to leave home. I learned HTML and created a web site to provide clean fun, opportunities for self-renewal, and a place to keep informed about news and events affecting baby boomers.

What's a typical day like at Boomers International?

"Getting emails from students, teachers and other boomers for help with research information (and sometimes opinions) about the boomer generation. Helping others find answers helps me broaden my knowledge as well. Balancing work, family and website, Maier says, "I can compartmentalize my life in a multi-task fashion, (just like a 32 bit computer)."

If I had to choose one reason why I enjoy my work so much it would have to be the opportunity to make someone happy, feel special. The world is a nicer place when people are happy.

READ MORE: www.boomersint.org
Photo Credit: Jeri Maier, USA.

Rita Golden Gelman

Photo Top: Rita on "the road" among newfound friends.
Photo Bottom: three of Rita's books written for children.

Rita Golden Gelman, ZOOMER™ February 2002

Hey, tough guy, think you've got a challenging and adventurous life?

Well, Rita Golden Gelman is a self-styled nomad with no permanent address and virtually no possessions.

Gelman has traveled the world for fifteen years, settling down temporarily in countries as varied as Mexico, Indonesia, and Thailand. A lifestyle like this one is definitely not for sissies.

These days, Gelman is taking her travel experiences "on the road" so to speak. Rita leads workshops on creativity and risk-taking. What kind of credentials does one need to teach that kind of workshop? Thirteen years of globe-trotting.

Gelman always wanted to "do life differently." The life of a nomad definitely has its challenges. "It was hard to be out of touch and almost unreachable.

I would write letters and send them off into space." It often took two or three weeks for her letters to reach their destination. Then it took another two weeks to answer back.

"E-mail changed my life" for the better, boasts the world traveler. Now days, Gelman communicates with family and friends as often as she wants.

At a time when most folk's lives are winding down, Gelman loves every minute of her adventurous lifestyle. "I take it a day at a time." She says, "I never thought about how long my journey would be. I just began.

The truth is, I try not to think too far ahead. Too much planning can stop you from doing what you really want to do. I have no idea what I'll be doing a year from now."

READ MORE: www.ritagoldengelman.com
Photo Credit: Fleishman-Hillard, USA.

Photo Top: running on empty road again
Photo Bottom: Running on Empty (L), mountain-biking (R)

Marshall Ulrich, ZOOMER™ May 2012

It's a bird? It's a plane? It's *Super Man !!!* Nope, wrong again. It's a ZOOMER, who just like yester-year's caped super-hero, is able to leap up tall mountains (climbing Everest) and can run faster than a speeding Boomer. Can you guess who this is? Well, as *Running Man*, Arnold Schwarzenegger might say, "It's naht a Boo-Mah."

Meet ZOOMER Marshall Ulrich, raised on a Colorado dairy farm, rising at dawn to do chores "seven days a week, before and after school, and all day Saturday, but Sunday afternoons were my own."

Now days, the once tractor-driving 8-year-old farm boy is called the "Endurance King" (*Outside* magazine). His publisher refers to this ultra-marathoner, adventure-runner, formidable-mountaineer as someone who possesses "an almost superman willpower."

Marshall's book, *Running on Empty* (Avery-Penguin, 2012) recounts his 3,063 mile run, at the tender age of 57, across the U.S.A. from sea-to-shining-sea. He is the first person to complete an unaided run across Death Valley to the top of Mount Whitney. He also ran in the Leadville 100, and the Pikes Peak Marathon. Now get this. He completed all these feats in ONE WEEKEND.

Running on Empty gives readers insights on how to ignite the powers of your mind to "go the distance." According to Marshall, "As you push your body beyond its limits, the mind can either help you or it can destroy you." He is "one of America's greatest living adventurers and without peer in human endurance," says Chris McDougall, author of *Born To Run*.

"The best I can figure is that we've been told too many times that adventure just isn't in the cards for everyday folk like you and me. Well, I'm not buying it" (Marshall Ulrich, *Running on Empty*, 2012).

READ MORE: www.MarshallUlrich.com
Photo Credit: Marshall Ulrich, USA.

These ZOOMERS, boomer with zip, illustrate the living proof that *"Retirement is the best time to stop acting your age, and start living your life."*

ZOOMER-FRIENDLY READING – OUTSIDE THE BOX

Running on Empty: running 3,063 miles in 52 days at age 57 Ulrich (2012).

Bill Gates Biography
www.biography.com/people/bill-gates-9307520

Steve Jobs
Isaacson (2011).

I Beat the Odds: Homelessness, to Blind Side, and Beyond Oher and Yaeger (2011).
Guinness World Records (ordinary heads - extraordinary feats)
www.guinnessworldrecords.com

Character Counts
Guinness (1999).

The Encyclopedia of Immaturity: how to never grow up, Klutz (2007).

3

Your Turn for a u-turn back to youth

Retirement is more a state of mind, than a stage of life.

Jeanne Calment rode her bike until age 110, and lived independently until 119. She loved eating chocolate, and drenched her meals with olive oil. She lived to age 122 years, at time when the average life expectancy was less than fifty years. Jeanne's longevity success story is the result of something more than just "smart genes and dumb luck." There is a science-based "yellow brick road" to longevity.

One million baby boomers are expected to live at least one hundred years (The Road to an Aging Policy for the 21st Century, WHCoA). Will you be one of the million? It depends on your answer to this question. "Does your longevity goal focus on slowing down your aging process, or preserving your youthful qualities?" There's a subtle, yet significant, difference between these two goals. In fact, your life depends on it.

There is an enormous amount of information about successful aging and active retirement, but it's too fragmented. Health experts write about fitness. Social scientists write about positive living. Retirement experts write about creating a financial nest egg for retirement. Finally, what information does exist is located throughout a maze of sources: medical centers, research institutes, universities, and pharmaceutical labs, all scattered around the globe.

This book helps the reader "connect the dots" between all the areas of expertise necessary to achieve a healthy, active, purposeful and secure retirement. The goal is to assemble all the pieces of the successful aging puzzle into one, unified longevity strategy I call Youth'n® that can be used, under the supervision of your health provider, to produce a longer, healthier, and active life.

Why should the experts be the only ones to own the inside track on longevity? This book levels the playing field, educating all who care to learn and apply the principles for successful aging. The result? Longevity will become an equal opportunity event, a choice to, or not to, act on the potential for life extension.

The fifty--plus age group is the fourth fastest growing segment of the population. Those age sixty-plus are the third fastest, those age seventy-plus are the second fastest, and those age eighty-plus are the fastest growing age group in the U.S.A.

In January 2011, the first boomers turned age 65, ushering in a new kind of older population, far removed from traditional stereotypes casting mature adults as passive, frail, and broke. The new older population will live a longer, healthier, and more prosperous retirement than any time in history.

Our youth-obsessed boomer population has created a huge demand for anti-aging products and services. As a result, consumers are constantly bombarded with an impressive menu of "must have" anti-aging diets, drugs, libido-enhancing drugs, age-erasing cosmetic cures, and the list goes on and on.

How do you keep up to date? How do you make sense of it all? What's valid information, and what's pop culture nonsense? It's enough to give you a mental hernia.

Time to end the frustration generated by conflicting information which leaves the average consumer wondering, "Why bother?" You can and will benefit from educating yourself, learning how to make practical, life-enhancing applications of youth-preservation strategies.

Growing your knowledge about youth-preservation is only half the battle. Putting that newfound knowledge to use depends on your attitude. In fact, your outlook can be your best friend or your worst enemy. Are you a "glass half empty" or a "glass half full" kind of person? That's an important question. Both the length and quality of your life depend on it. Optimists age like wine. Pessimists age like milk. Why you age is up to nature. How you age is up to you.

Anyone searching for instant miracle cures, an all-in-one anti-aging pill, or non-scientific solutions based on personal testimonials and secret remedies "not available in stores" (because retail stores have standards) will not find much to their liking in this book. Instead, readers are introduced to scientifically valid youth-preservation research.

This book's review of literature on aging and retirement is confined to trustworthy sources such as findings reported in peer-reviewed journals and scientific reports authored by experts who possess the appropriate academic credentials necessary to speak with authority on their respective topic.

Your search for knowledge must take into account the sources of that knowledge. There are rules of thumb that can help filter and fine-tune your sources of information. For example, nutritionists and dieticians offer advice on food and diets. However, the title "dietician" is professionally regulated. Individuals must be certified and licensed in order to use the "dietician" title. However, use of the title "nutritionist" is less regulated, offering no guarantee of expertise.

The title, "gerontologist" is another example of an unregulated title. For example, I hold a PhD from the University of Michigan with certifications in Aging, Geriatric Assessment, Milieu Therapy, and Retirement Planning. I am a "gerontologist." However, that title is also used by individuals with little or no formal training. Again, the point is to identify your sources of information if you want to be sure that you're reading fact, not fabrication.

Sometimes there are two valid, conflicting points of view on the same topic or issue. That's because the Aging Enterprise consists of two different types of communities. The scientific community (a.k.a. Ivory Tower) focuses on the creation of aging knowledge. The business community (a.k.a. Wall Street) focuses on profitable applications of that knowledge, marketing products and services promising to improve the day-to-day lives of consumers.

This tug-of-war relationship between Wall Street and the Ivory Tower is simultaneously symbiotic, antagonistic, and necessary. How's that for irony? Surprised? Don't be. Read on.

The Ivory Tower of academia is deliberately cautious about relying on only preliminary research findings. It's better to wait on confirmation from follow-up studies, a prudent, yet lengthy process. However, the business community responds to market forces. Consumers are impatient. They read about advances in anti-aging research and want to avail themselves to those breakthroughs now, not later.

Consumer demand creates a race between competitors who battle to dominate a marketplace of seventy-eight million boomers who believe their time on earth is running out, and spend billions of dollars on products that promise to cheat Father Time. As a result, age-phobic boomers don't want to wait decades for results of follow-up research studies necessary to confirm the efficacy of anti-aging product claims.

The FDA has long-surrendered to consumer demands for supplements. Today, just about any anti-aging product can be sold as long as the product label states, "The product claims have not been evaluated by the FDA." In response to the FDA's turn-a-blind-one policy, the both the National Research Council and Institute of Medicine are creating a framework for the FDA to systematically evaluate the public health consequences of its decisions concerning the approval of food supplements and prescription products (National Academy of Science, 2011).

Even with the arsenal of anti-aging knowledge, the reader should keep this fact in mind. Research statistics do not "prove" anything. Instead, researchers report only the level of significance and level of confidence in their findings. There is always the probability, however small, that research findings may have occurred simply by chance variance, meaning the reported research findings may not be true.

Of course, the higher the level of confidence a researcher has that his findings are not due to chance, the greater the value of the research findings. In addition, future research might question, tomorrow, what we believe to true today about a particular health supplement. Sometimes, science "throws in the towel" by approving a health product that has known health hazards. As a case in point, the FDA is considering the approval of a previously disapproved weight-loss supplement because the incidence of obesity is rising out of control.

Reminds me of today's prescription ads promoting a drug that will reduce your stomach pain, but the side-effects of the drug can cause head pain, back aches and even death. We are addicted to our medicine cabinets. Wouldn't it be better to practice prevention in order to lower our health risks in the first place?

HOMEWORK ASSIGNMENT

If you haven't visited your public library in a while, you are in for a pleasant surprise. Libraries have gone high-tech and librarians are highly skilled experts at sourcing information. Visit your local public library and ask to review either print or online copies of "peer-reviewed" journals reporting on health and aging research. You will know the studies are peer-reviewed because the research journal will say so. Peer-reviewed means a team of researchers have determined the author's methodology and findings have scientific merit.

Trade magazines, on the other hand, offer articles that may be based on hard science, or may be biased opinions of the author. Such articles provide thought-provoking reading, but there is no guarantee of scientific merit. The article may be an "advertorial" which is an article authored by an "advertiser" who is not submit to the peer-review process. Advertorials promote products or services just like an advertisement, but in a narrative form that does not appear to be an advertisement.

Start empowering yourself to live a longer, healthier, active lifestyle. A list of prominent journals is provided at the back of this book. When you find a journal of interest, "Google" the journal title online for access to the research articles. Do what journalists do. Check the sources of information to ensure accuracy.

Surfing the Internet is a tremendous resource for information of all kinds. Remember, web site addresses are instructive. Web domains ending in ".gov" are sponsored by local, state or federal government. Web addresses ending in ".org" tend to be sponsored by professional and scientific not-for-profit associations. But beware. Many of these sites accept advertising. So, it is possible that the web site information might be biased in support of the web site's advertisers.

Webs ending in ".edu" are educational institutions: K-12, college or university. An .edu web site may be non-profit or for-profit. Be sure to read the About Us section the web site.

The ".com" web sites range from "excellent" to "suspect" sources of information. Reading material originating from these web sites require that you check the academic credentials of the authors. Be sure to use multiple web sources to cross-reference your reading. When in doubt, log-on to the National Institutes of Health, NIH.gov to cross-check the validity of information found on the Internet.

Here's how two sources of knowledge can conflict, even though the sources are both medical doctors. A prominent online medical doctor advocates so-called anti-aging regimens that are at odds with medical science research. Example one: medical research reports that cancer (oral, throat, lung) and psychological disorders are associated with marijuana use. Yet, one of the doctor's book states that moderate use of pot can extend your life. Example two: book promotes substantial weight-loss within just one week, but medical science reports that weight-loss strategy is known to increase cardio-vascular, obesity and metabolic health risks. Before you plunge into any health strategy, remember, it's you, not the doctor, who is going to die if and when things go terribly wrong.

Life is short, but you can stretch it. So, let's get started. Log-on to the free "Life-Stretcher Quiz" to identify both the plus-factors (your personal strengths) and negative-factors (your inherited health-risks) that will predict your life-expectancy. Many such calculators exist on the internet these days, with one thing in common. They are all inaccurate, some just a bit, others to a fault. It would require a thorough physical examination, lab work and stress tests to approximate an accurate prediction of life expectancy. Then again, you could pass your health examination with flying colors, only to get hit by a bus on your way home from the doctor's office. So what is the value of life-expectancy calculators? Calculators raise your awareness about the multitude of interdisciplinary factors that determine how well and how long you will live.

Longevity is a multifaceted, team sport (working with your health provider) to adopt a total fitness lifestyle: monitoring inherited health risks, exercising your body and mind, sound nutrition and diet and a sense of purpose. Here's the point, longevity calculators offer an entertaining way to learn about wellness and differentiate your chronological age from your real age (Calculate Your Age in Neo-Years, Demko 1980. AgeVentureNewsService.com/neoyear.htm).

ZOOMER-FRIENDLY READING – LIMITLESS LIVING

The Longest Life - Jeanne Calment
Allard, Calment et al (1998).

STAY YOUNGER LONGER: take the life-stretcher quiz
www.demko.com/life-stretcher-quiz.htm (1976-2012)

LIFE IS SO GOOD: One Man's Extraordinary Journey through the 20th Century and how he learned to Read at Age 98
Dawson and Glaubman (2001).

The Blue Zones: Lessons for Living Longer From the People Who've Lived the Longest
Buettner (2010).

The Half-Lived Life: Overcoming Passivity and Rediscovering Your Authentic Self
Lee (2012).

Called to Coach: Reflections on Life, Faith and Football
Bowden (2011).

4

FOOD FITNESS: EAT YOUR WAY TO BETTER HEALTH

Zoomers adhere to a nutritional and caloric dietary plan based on functional age, gender, BMI and level of activity.

"*90% of Americans say their diet is healthy,*" (ConsumerReports. org, 2011). Hmm. Would that be "healthy" as in "I maintain my ideal weight?" No. Fifty-seven percent were actually overweight or clinically obese. Hmm, would that be "healthy" as in "I'm eating a balanced diet?" No. Only 1 in 4 Americans consume adequate (three) servings of fruits and vegetables daily, even though a diet high in fruits and vegetables can reduce the risk for many leading causes of death (CDC, 2010). Here's the point. "90 percent of Americans *only imagine* their diet is healthy."

GIGO. That's computer slang for "Garbage In, Garbage Out." It means when you enter bad (garbage) data into your computer, you get back "garbage" results. There's a lesson here for all of us. "What you eat might be the very thing that's eating you."

Every time you fill your car's gas tank, there is a choice to be made about the grade of fuel you use (regular, special, or super). Ever wonder how much better your car might run if you started feeding it a higher grade of fuel, a better quality of energy?

You don't have to be a rocket scientist to figure out that healthy eating is a matter of balancing caloric intake with your level of activity, gender and age. I call this Healthy InSide - Healthy Outside (HI-HO ... hi-ho, it's off to health we go).

Let's get started with some common sense, research-based guidelines. The body requires a reasonable amount of calories in order to breathe, circulate blood, digest food, maintain posture, be physically active and to sleep (yes, you burn calories while sleeping).

On January 31, 2011, USDA released the 2010 Dietary Guidelines for Americans. Unlike the smoke-and-mirrors approach used by quick-weight-loss programs, the USDA recommendations are based on research known to promote health. Adults are encouraged to consume more vegetables, fruits, whole grains, fat-free and low-fat dairy products and seafood and to consume less sodium, saturated fats, trans fats, sugar and refined grains. These are just the broad strokes. Read on and learn specific steps for living a more healthy, active and longer life.

YOUTH'N UP YOUR FOOD-FITNESS IQ

Here's what the research says about food fitness.

1. How many calories do you need in order to maintain your weight? Multiply your weight in pounds by 15. The answer equals the number of calories your body requires each day. The American

Dietetic Association (www.EatRight.org) will help you determine the number of calories you need each day based on your chronological age, gender and activity level. For example, a 50 year old woman requires on average, 2,100 calories daily. A 50 year old male requires an average of 2,600 calories per day.

2. Find out whether you need to raise, retain, or lose body weight? Get an answer by calculating your Body Mass Index (BMI), a comparison of body height and weight.

BMI is reported as one-of-four scores:

18 or less =   BMI is below average (you are underweight)
18.5 - 24.9 =   BMI is in normal-range (retain your weight)
25 to 29.9 =   BMI is above average (lose weight)
30 or more =   BMI indicates clinical obesity (see your doctor ASAP)
Calculate your BMI for free at: www.nhlbisupport.com/BMI

3. Expand meal time to a full thirty minutes, which is the amount of time your brain needs to send the body the signal to "stop eating."

BTW, the average meal is completed in less than 7 minutes. Here's the point. You remain "hungry" for the remaining 23 minutes, prompting you to keep eating.

5. The most successful (take it off and keep it off) weight-loss goal is one-pound-per-week. Avoid all those nonsensical "lose 7 pounds in 5 days" diets, many advocated by medical doctors who should know better than dispense whacky advice that flies in the face of medical science.

6. One pound of body weight is equal to 3,500 calories. In order to lose one pound of body weight (not just water weight), reduce your weekly caloric intake by 3,500 calories, 500 calories each day for 7 days.

7. Quick-fix diets typically result in gaining back all weight lost, and often gaining a few pounds more. Healthy lifestyle and sound eating habits will keep the weight off better than binge and purge dieting.

8. Hydration. "Drink 6-8 glasses of water a day." NO, NOT REALLY! That kind of "one size fits all" advice is like saying one

prescription of eyeglasses fits everyone. Add a little science to your hydration needs. Divide your body weight in pounds by 2 which is equal to your daily water requirement in ounces. If you exercise, you will need another 10 ounces of water for every half-hour of activity. I start each morning with a tall (12 oz) glass of water before breakfast or coffee because my body needs to hydrate after sleeping eight hours. So, drink water first before that first cup of coffee. If you are a tea-drinker that's even better because certain teas have been proven to hydrate the body faster than just pure water.

9. How hungry would you be if you had not eaten for 8 hours? Well, that's why breakfast is so important because when you awake in the morning, your body has not received any nutrients in the past eight or nine hours. You need to refill your tank before starting your engine. Seventy-five percent of all successful dieters eat breakfast, typically consisting of some cereal and fruit. So, don't skip the most important meal of the day.

Let's get acquainted with your body's energy sources: food groups and daily requirements. Food choices are often made on the basis of taste, not nutritional value. Here are a few questions that help get you up-to-speed on food fitness. What's the difference between vitamins and minerals? What foods and nutrients qualify for "organic" status? Is there a real difference between organic vitamins and non-organic vitamins? What qualifies as a dietary "supplement," and what exactly does it supplement?

It's important that you are able to answer these questions because the FDA is not watching out for health food shoppers these days. The labels on dietary supplements carry this warning: "These statements (product claims made by the manufacturer) have not been evaluated by the Food and Drug Administration. This product is not intended to diagnose, treat, cure, or prevent any disease." Hmmm, that sounds like "you are on your own" when it comes to food choices. So you better know the answers or you're gambling with your health; rolling the dice or using a dartboard to decide what to put into your body. When it comes to managing the foods that energize your body, you're the one in the driver's seat.

NUTRITION TERMINOLOGY

Before going on, it's important to define a few key terms. A **nutrient** is a biochemical found in food that provides the body with energy and building materials to sustain life. Nutrients have seven classifications: water, vitamins, minerals, carbohydrates, fats, and proteins. These are defined below.

Water. The definitions of "pure water" are wide and varied. According to www.freedrinkingwater.com, "The bacteriologist is apt to regard "pure water" as a sterile liquid, that is, one with no living bacteria in it. The chemist, on the other hand, might well classify water as "pure" when it possesses no mineral, gaseous or organic impurities." The moral of this story? The "S" in the word Science does not stand for "Simple Explanation." U.S. EPA standards help regulate the safety of your tap water, and the U.S. FDA regulates the standard of quality found in bottled water. By the way, did you know that 50% of all water bottled in the U.S. is not "spring" water as many brand labels state (Consumer Reports, 2011)?

Vitamins are organic substances that help regulate the body's metabolism (your body's energy engine). Vitamins do not provide the body with energy or building blocks. The job of a vitamin is to trigger those processes. Just like a key, a vitamin starts the car, initiating the processes of movement, reliability and speed. Vitamins are either water-soluble (voided daily by the body) or fat-soluble (stored in body fat) and as a result, fat-soluble vitamins can reach high levels of toxicity, causing illness and death because the body keeps storing larger and larger amounts in body fat. "Too much of a good thing is NOT a good thing."

RDA suggests which vitamins and dosages are necessary for normal growth, reproductive power, and maintenance of health. Pay attention to the percentages listed. Vitamins administered in excess of the RDA (100%) should be considered therapeutic dosages that only a medical doctor should prescribe. Also, beware of "celebrity" doctors who gobble handfuls of pills throughout the day, professing miraculous health benefits. If you saw these doctors up-close you might think they are very ill or terminal, rather than in a state of "robust health" as claimed.

A word of caution. Your diet may contain all the vitamins necessary for your age, gender, BMI and level of activity. However, some bodies are not able to adequately absorb ingested vitamins, such as adults with diabetes or other hormonal disorders. So, it's prudent to have a physician and registered dietician monitor your body's nutrient intake, then analyze your blood chemistry to make sure your body is able to absorb the nutrients you ingest. Don't guess. Get checked.

Minerals are twenty-one inorganic substances (unlike vitamins that are organic) and are classified into six groups. Although "minerals only make up a small percentage (5%) of body weight, their role in the body is significant and life would not be possible without them" (www.expert-nutrition.com/minerals.html, 2012).

Minerals are essential for growth of muscle and bones, body metabolism and ensuring the healthy function of cells, tissues and organ systems. Examples of minerals: calcium, sodium, potassium iron, phosphorus. A bone-density test, for example, might detect harmful effects of a calcium deficiency, a condition common among adult women, but can also be found in men.

What kinds and amounts of minerals does your body require? The USDA Daily Nutrient Calculator (fnic.nal.usda.gov/interactive DRI) calculates your daily nutrient needs based on what is called the Dietary Reference Intakes (DRIs). The calculator represents the most current scientific knowledge on nutrient needs, developed by the National Academy of Science's Institute of Medicine. Log-on to the calculator to estimate your daily requirement for 21 minerals, based on your age, gender, height, weight and level of activity.

Carbohydrates provide energy to the body in the form of sugar. Sugar is available in two forms: simple and complex. Simple sugar (glucose) offers readily available energy. Complex sugar (polysaccharides) such as starch and fiber release energy more slowly throughout the body. This is why a high-sugar breakfast cereal can leave you literally starving for another energy-boost around mid-morning. On the other hand, an oatmeal and banana breakfast "stays with you longer" and hunger returns closer to lunch time.

Good sources of sugar-energy come from complex carbohydrates such as bananas and apples which take longer to digest, allowing the sugar to be slowly released over a long period of time. Simple sugars like cake and candy are quickly digested, releasing the energy in short bursts, creating bursts of energy which quickly drops as your body works to re-balance the high level of sugar in your blood.

Healthy blood-glucose levels are maintained by the interaction of insulin and glucose. Insulin is a hormone produced by your pancreas the bonds with glucose in the bloodstream. Glucose is then transported throughout the body to tissues and cells as an energy source. Insulin, on the other hand, helps keep your blood-sugar at a healthy level, not too low or too high.

Fats are another energy source, but play the additional roles of insulating and cushioning the body, and helping absorb fat-soluble vitamins (A, D, E, K, carotenoids). Fats consumed as food are combinations of monounsaturated, polyunsaturated, and saturated fatty acids. Saturated fats can raise your risk to high blood pressure, obesity, diabetes, and heart disease. That is why saturated fats are referred to as "bad cholesterol" (LDL). Unsaturated fats (HDL) are beneficial. They include polyunsaturated fats, and monounsaturated fats, and are found in vegetable oil, nuts, olives, avocados and salmon.

Remember. Do not eliminate fat from your diet (unless directed to do so by your physician). Cholesterol is essential for your body to produce hormones and vitamins. Choose your fat intake wisely. Keep saturated fats to a minimum. Palm oil, palm kernel oil, and coconut oil are primarily saturated fat, but not cholesterol.

The American Heart Association provides an excellent presentation about dietary fat called Fat 101. Log-on to www.heart.org to learn more.

Protein is found in every living cell of the body. Proteins from meat are considered "complete" proteins because they supply all of the amino acids the body can't make on its own. Plant proteins are incomplete. "The human body requires 50-65 grams of protein daily" (www.nlm.nih.gov/medlineplus/dietaryproteins.html).

"Proteins are molecules that contain twenty types of amino acids linked to one another in long chains. The specific function of each protein is determined by how the amino amino acids are sequenced (ordered) within a chain. That is why proteins are categorized into five groups based on how each group functions in the body" (NIH, National Library of Medicine).

1. *Antibodies* are proteins that protect the body from invading viruses and bacteria.
2. *Enzyme proteins* are catalysts that initiate chemical reactions within the body's cells which are essential to life itself.
3. *Messenger proteins* are like traffic cops, directing signals that coordinate the biological processes between cells, tissues, and organs.
4. *Structural proteins* function like the infrastructure of a house, giving form and providing support for the cells. Without this structure, it would be impossible to move your body in any direction.
5. *Genomes* refer to all of the biological information needed to build and maintain the body. This information is stored in your DNA where genes instruct each type of body cell (such as skin cells, brain cells, liver cells) to create all the unique proteins necessary to sustain life. This process is called "genetic expression."

MY STORY

"Such a nice, healthy child," my grandmother boasted as she pinched my chubby cheeks and twisted them rosy-red. A plump child was a healthy child. This was an indisputable "truth" during the first twenty years of my "clean-your-plate-because-people-elsewhere-are-starving" life. By the seventh grade, I weighed 157 pounds and carried a five-sandwich lunch tucked under my plump arm. Two years later, I tried out for high school football, and the varsity squad trampled my weight down to 119 pounds. I was now known as "Beanpole," but not for long. By my sophomore year in college, I weighed in at 233 pounds. This fat-thin-fat-thin-fat seesaw life did not cease until I learned a thing or two about food, nutrition, diets, and dieting.

GET YOUTH TO YOUR AGE: in six quick steps

Are your food choices based on sight or science? Common sense, and determination will help you establish and maintain a healthy body weight and a nutritious diet. Assess your needs based on the following six steps toward health-maintenance (below). Then, if major changes in your food habits are necessary, move on and review the dietary options (discussed later) available to fit your unique needs and get you back on track.

Step 1: Calculate your Body Mass Index (BMI)
Here's how to make that decision, in partnership with your health provider, of course. Body Mass Index (BMI) is a measure of your body fat, based on height and weight. BMI applies to both adult men and women. For an exact calculation of BMI (standard and metric) and interpretation of your BMI score, consult the NHLBI Web site at http://www.nhlbisupport.com/bmi/.

Step 2: Calculate your caloric needs
Now, determine how many daily calories you need to maintain your current weight. Multiply your weight in pounds times 1.5. This gives you the number of calories you need per day. Example: If you weigh 160 pounds, you need to consume 2,400 calories per day.

Step 3: Weight reduction versus calorie reduction
First, set a reasonable weight-loss goal. In order to lose one pound, reduce your caloric intake by 3,500 calories over a reasonable length of time of about two weeks.

Sound like a slow way to lose weight? Perhaps. But the goal is to lose weight and keep it off. Crash dieters gain back every pound. Keep to no more than a 10 percent daily reduction in calories. A 10 percent daily calorie reduction for a 160-pound person (240 calories) results in the loss of one pound (3,500 calories) in fourteen days.

Step 4: Hydrate your body
Drinking sufficient amounts of water is essential to your health. Especially if you live in a hot, sub-tropical, or tropical climate because you run a higher risk of developing kidney stones due to insufficient hydration. Divide your weight in pounds by two. The answer equals the daily number of ounces of water you need. A 150-pound person requires 75 ounces of water per day.

Step 5: Eat breakfast
A national survey by Consumer Reports found that every successful
diet plan recommends that you eat breakfast. Here's why. Seventy-five
percent of all successful dieters eat breakfast, typically some cereal and
fruit.

Step 6: Timing is everything
Be patient. Take time to learn about nutrition, dieting, exercise, and
how to modify your eating habits. This will enable you to choose, if
needed, the right weight-management (diet) plan to fit your personal
needs.

EIGHT WEIGHT-MANAGEMENT CONCEPTS

Want to know how most Americans address the problem of being
overweight? They feel that as long as they are doing something
about it, they have an excuse for being fat. I'm sure you've heard
someone say, "I'm trying to lose," as they retrieve another handful
of bread sticks from the center of the restaurant table. As long as
they are doing something and that something includes merely
thinking about their weight problem, they believe their overeating
is acceptable. That's why many Americans continue to gain weight
because they are "doing something about it," like making payments
on a piece of exercise equipment they never use. There are plenty
of dietary options available to those of us who are "horizontally
challenged."

Let's face it. Losing weight is a no-brainer. Keeping those pounds
off isn't as easy. The first thing you need to do is understand how and
why your diet plan is supposed to work. Then, choose a plan you can
incorporate into your lifestyle (like taking the stairs instead of the
elevator). Otherwise, whatever plan you choose, it will not work, no
matter how spectacular. What's worse, many failed dieters gain back
all pounds lost, and sometimes even more added weight.

Keep in mind that diets are risky business. That's why the
National Institutes of Health categorized various types of diets
based on the goal the dieter wants to achieve such weight-loss,

weight-gain, controlling diabetes, or avoiding hazardous elements like sodium, saturated fats, to name a few. A registered dietician is best qualified to offer advice based on your unique needs identified by your doctor.

1. Fixed-menu diets

This diet focuses on a limited list of foods you are restricted to eat.

PRO: This kind of diet is easy to follow because the foods are selected for you.

CON: Because food choices are limited, the diet may get boring and hard to follow, especially when away from home. In addition, fixed-menu diets do not teach the food-selection skills necessary for keeping weight off. If you start with a fixed-menu diet, you should eventually switch to a plan that helps you learn to make meal choices on your own, such as an exchange-type diet, described below.

2. Exchange-type diets

This diet is a meal plan that focuses on the number of servings from each of several food groups. Within each group, foods are about equal in calories and can be interchanged as you wish. For example, the "starch" category could include one slice of bread or half a cup of oatmeal; each is about equal in nutritional value and calories.

PRO: You have day-to-day variety and you can easily follow the diet away from home. Best benefit is the plan teaches food selection skills necessary to keep your weight off.

CON: Mealtime requires a focus on analysis of types and portions, calling attention to diet when you just want to socialize or relax.

3. Pre-packaged-meal diets

This plan focuses on the presentation of appropriate portion sizes, and gives you everything food-wise that you need.

PRO: Meal planning and calorie counting is a No-Brainer, and you get a 3-D image of what a healthy meal should look like.

CON: Requires purchase of prepackaged meals that are often costly. May not teach you how to select and prepare food. What do you do with the remaining boxful of meals if you hate the taste or texture?

4. Formula diets

The focus is on short-term, results-oriented weight loss by substituting one or more meals with a liquid, powder, pill or meal-bar substitute.

PRO: Provides a balanced diet containing a mix of protein, carbohydrates, and usually a small amount of fat. The plans are easy to follow and often result in rapid weight loss.

CON: Rapid weight loss is not healthy, and most people regain the weight as soon as they stop using the formula. In addition, formula diets do not teach the skills needed for keeping weight off.

5. Questionable (Miracle) diets

The focus is on a "Miracle pill or drug" that is "not available in stores" (perhaps, because STORES have STANDARDS). You should avoid any diet that suggests a certain nutrient or food to promote easy weight loss.

PRO: Some of these diets may work in the short term because they are low in calories.

CON: These diets may not be well balanced, causing nutrient deficiencies. In addition, they do not teach eating habits that are important for long-term weight management. Evidence in support of the product anecdotal (results not typical) rather than based on scientific clinical trials. Miracles do happen … in heaven, but you have to die to get there!

6. Flexible diets

The focus is on monitoring "one factor" such as fat only, calories only, or a combination of the two, with the individual making the choice of both the type and amount of food eaten.

PRO: Teaches which foods to avoid or control for weight management..
CON: Does not address a dieter's total dietary needs. The plan does not teach food-selection skills for weight loss or weight maintenance.

7. Appetite Reduction Diets

The focus is on choosing a food that directly controls hunger. Remember the age-old remedies for weight-loss? Drink a glass of water before or with your meal. Eat a teaspoon of peanut butter when you get the urge to snack. Drink a glass of grapefruit juice to

reduce your appetite. These appetite reduction strategies have been branded in new programs like SENSA® and the FULLBAR®. Both are intended to reduce your appetite, resulting in weight-loss.
PRO: Effective short-term weight loss strategy.
CON: Does not address the metabolic mechanisms that control the frequency or causes of hyper-appetite.

8. Lifestyle Diets
There are a few more resources that pick up where earlier diet programs left off. They all address the issue of diet failure—that people eventually "end" their diet plan and gain all the weight back. I call this approach the new "lifestyle diets" because the focus is on permanently changing the way people eat, as well as, energizing their changing lifestyle (calorie-burning) habits. Dieting alone just doesn't work because that strategy means you must stay of a "diet" for life. The lifestyle diets reinvent the whole concept of diet—that people need a new and healthy way of eating and living. Why? Consumers never need to "get off" the lifestyle diet, because it isn't really a diet at all. You won't wonder anymore when you should "start" the diet or how long you have to stay on it before you go "off."

Use the eight weight-loss concepts to evaluate a lifestyle diet that is right for you. Forget the hype in the diet-plan advertisements and go with the science behind the product. Examples of what I call lifestyle diet plans include the following. This is not an all-inclusive list, nor is it a rank-ordered list. Just examples of what I believe address the Lifestyle (permanent) weight management diet.

A. Bull's Eye Diet
Author, Josephine Connolly Schoonen, a registered dietician says, "Rather than focusing on weight loss, decide to manage your weight over time. Taking on this goal and the associated necessary self-education will empower you to make dramatic improvements in your health and weight."

B. Volumetric Weight-Control Plan
Author, Barbara Rolls, PhD, explains that a "volumetric" approach to weight management is based on caloric density of foods and a sense of

feeling full, enables people to lose weight and keep it off while eating satisfying portions of delicious food.

C. Diet Power Weight-Loss Coach
This third resource is not a diet, but a computer program that works independently, or in concert with Atkins, South Beach, Weight Watchers, and the American Heart Association Diet. This tool provides daily analysis of food consumed, level of activity, and body weight to monitor your progress and adjust your food intake.

D. Energy-balanced Diet
The U.S. Department of Agriculture (USDA) provides guidelines for eating based on your energy needs. The USDA believes that adopting this balanced eating pattern is a good way to match lifestyle with dietary needs. Examples of this diet can be accessed at the USDA Food Guide.

E. The Fresh Start Thermogenic Diet
Author Cathi Graham explains that thermogenic foods "are fat-burning foods that naturally speed up your metabolism, help burn calories, and help you lose weight no matter what your body type." Examples of fat-burning foods are salsa, celery, salmon, chicken, almonds, and green tea. Graham, once diagnosed as "morbidly obese," lost 186 pounds following her special diet.

F. The Dash Diet
Author, Marla Heller's DASH Diet explains how to incorporate healthy eating a dietary plan for people with busy lifestyles. The plan offers expert opinions from a registered dietician on how to make convenient, tasty, and healthy food choices regardless of schedules and time.

HAZARDS OF PORTION DISTORTION
Anyone eating on the run or in restaurants has probably noticed that food portions have gotten larger. Some portions are called "super-size," while others have simply grown in size and provide enough food for at

least two people. With this growth have come increases in waistlines and body weight.

To see if you know how today's portions compare to earlier portion estimates, visit the Web site at: http://hin.nhlbi.nih.gov/portion/. You can quiz yourself on Portion Distortion I and II.

See the Internet links at the Self-help Resources section at the end of this chapter. You will also learn about the amount of physical activity required to burn off the extra calories provided by today's portions.

A FINAL WORD

One-third of all Americans are on a diet at any given time. Two-thirds who manage to lose weight end up gaining all the pounds back, sometimes more. This explains why there are lots of diet strategies, many of which never work. The perfect (one-size-fits-all) diet plan has yet to be discovered. There are different diets based on your food fitness goals.

ZOOMER-FRIENDLY READING – FOOD FITNESS

USDA Dietary Guidelines
www.dietaryguidelines.gov

Super Foods Rx: 14 Foods Will Change Your Life
Straten and Griggs (2006).

Superfoods: 101 Best Foods to Live Longer, Feel Younger
Millwood Media (2011).

Supplements – Facts and Precautions
Dietary and Herbal Supplements, U. S. National Institutes of Health
Website: nccam.nih.gov/health/supplements/wiseuse.htm#sources

Food Dyes – Facts and Cautions
Food Dyes: a Rainbow of Risks – Center for Science in the Public Interest (2010). www.cspinet.org

Menu Planning
http://hin.nhlbi.nih.gov/menuplanner/menu.cgi

Portion Management
Portion Distortion Quiz: http://hin.nhlbi.nih.gov/portion

Special Diet: for hypertension
DASH Diet Action Plan Heller (2011).

Special Diet: for diabetes
The Mayo Clinic Diabetes Diet, Mayo Clinic Experts (2011).

The Mayo Clinic Diet
Weight-loss Experts at Mayo Clinic (2010).

Weight-Loss Diets – Facts and Cautions
Consumer Reports Diet Survey (2007).
www.consumerreports.org

Are We Fooling Ourselves?
90 percent of Americans say their diet is healthy.

ConsumerReports.org (2011).

5

COGNITIVE FITNESS: WHEN YOUR BRAIN WAVES, "GOODBYE"

Zoomers perform daily brain exercises (neurobics) to sustain memory, learning, and problem-solving skills.

*D*o *you worry about your memory? Go blank on names and faces? Enter a room, and then forget what you came in for? Congratulations, you're normal.* (Reader's Digest, circa 1970). We all associate these cognitive problems (memory, learning, and thinking) with the aging process. The truth is, most of the time, these cognitive problems have nothing to do with your age, and are completely reversible conditions. Here's the point. *People retire, minds don't.*

BRAIN FITNESS FACTS

Here's what the research says about brain fitness.

➢ Memory loss (short-term and long term) is not an inevitable part of the normal aging process.

➢ The six most common causes of cognitive decline in mature adults are reversible.

➢ Both high and low blood pressure can decrease memory skills and ability to concentrate.

➢ Reading aloud, solving puzzles, and playing a musical instrument can lower your risk to dementia.

➢ Alzheimer's risk is reduced by healthy diet, aerobics, intellectual activity, and socializing.

➢ Senile dementia refers to late-life problems with memory, learning, and problem-solving.

➢ Senile psychosis refers to late-life problems with personality and mood disorders.

➢ Research on human potential has identified at least eight distinct types of intelligence.

➢ Neurobics is the name given to mental exercises that promote healthy brain function.

"Use it, or lose it." Cognitive skills that have been dormant for years can be revitalized. How? Brain exercises called neurobics. Chances are you have already used neurobics without knowing it. Card games, learning a language, crossword puzzles, chess and learning to play a musical instrument are all examples of neurobics.

Johns Hopkins' University reports that memory training is increasingly important with age because the brain's ability to "file" new information often results in forgetting recent events like where you parked your car, left your car keys or remembering the name of someone you just met (Proceedings of the National Academy of Science, May 2011). The study's author, JHU Neuroscience Professor, Michael Yassa reports, "the hippocampus, the area of the brain that stores memories, becomes degraded over time … (as a result) our brains cannot accurately file new information." As we get older, explains Yassa, interference from older memories interferes with the ability to recall recent events. He thinks that is also why, "We tend to reminisce so much more when we get older because it is easier to recall old memories than make new ones."

Here's the point. Memory changes with age, but there are a variety of techniques for improvement with the use of neurobics, brain exercise. This newfound discovery of the brain's plasticity has prompted organizations like the American Association of Community Colleges (2011 AACC "Plus 50 Completion Strategy") to continue as well as expand a successful three-year project that get boomers back into the classroom, completing degrees and certificate programs. It's never too late to refresh your learning skills. What once was lost can often be recaptured.

Seventy-eight million boomers are candidates for educational programs that offer skill-refreshers and second career opportunities, providing the economy with productive, reliable, mature employees. One 50-plus coed reports, "I think it keeps you young because I've met so many wonderful people going through different phases in their lives" (Inside Higher Ed, April 27, 2011). The flood of boomers to campus is what Yogi Berra might call, "Déjà Vu, all over again."

MY STORY

I didn't really learn to read until I graduated from college. You see, there are many different levels of reading comprehension, as I later learned. Some people quickly glance at traffic signs and billboards, sprint through newspapers and magazines, slowly move through a much-loved novel, or spend hours reading a contract. Yes, there are many types of reading styles. My problem was I had only one reading style: slow, very slow.

I was always a painfully slow reader. Books that others completed in an afternoon, took me days and days to read. But not anymore. I learned, and now practice, many levels of reading comprehension depending on the nature of the material and my goal for reading it in the first place. I realized that I needed to change my style …"some day" (which is code for "probably never").

Eventually the opportunity to improve found me a few years later when I recommended one of my (slow reader) students to visit the college's Teaching-Learning Center (TLC) for tutoring. As my student began taking a reading assessment test, the TLC director tried to put the student at ease by saying, "How about if Professor Demko goes first to show how easy the reading test is." Terror struck me. If I took the test, everyone would discover my reading problem. Well, I toughed it out, took the assessment test, and learned how to read, truly read…for the first time. Improvement is never easy, but always good.

Decades later, a driver collided with my car. I didn't wake up until a week later. Cognitive problems? Yes, I had to learn how to read again. A page full of words looked like a tossed salad. Learning how to drive again took months because I could see that the traffic light was red or green, but I had no clue what the color meant, stop or go or just sit there and wonder. My disability had a bonus, however. A family friend owned a Limo service and I got chauffeured to work every day for a month. It was wonderful. As the embarrassingly long Limo approached the college campus, I waved to an adoring crowd of students, who greeted me like a Rock Star, "Puff Davey."

Everyone has an intellectual shortcoming that, on the surface, appears to be irreversible. We think we're slow-minded, senile, or just plain stupid. Worst of all, we sometimes accept "our fate," convincing ourselves that we are damaged goods. Never mind how we got there, there's nothing we can do to improve, so we just stop trying. It been fourteen years since "the accident" and there are good days and bad days. It's no big deal anymore because I am alive to talk about it. Cheating death is a great liberator. It teaches you to not sweat the small stuff and not take the miracles of life for granted. Wow, I am so lucky to have had that cognitive awakening. Rain, snow, clouds? No problem. Every day above ground is a good one.

The same genius mind that enabled Einstein to comprehend the Theory of Relativity was the same mind that caused him to forget something as simple as his phone number. On one occasion, Einstein "forgot" to put on his pants when he left home. It was only absent-mindedness. We remember what's important.

INTELLECTUAL FITNESS

Starting a brain-fitness regimen does not have to be a hassle. Simple neurobic exercises can be incorporated into your daily routine in order to tune-up your cognitive skills and boost your brain power. As a case in point, clinical research (Kawashima, 2005; Gamon and Gragdon, 2004; Gardner, 2000) all demonstrated the fluid nature of an individual's brain power. Starting today, incorporate mental tasks into your daily routine. Right-handed? Use your left-hand to brush your teeth or comb your hair. Use audio-CDs to learn and practice a new language while carpooling to work.

Writing in Making Music Magazine (www.makingmusicmag. com 2005), Dr. William Umiker reported on a study of older adults participating in group keyboard lessons which discovered increased levels of human growth hormone, known to prevent such aging phenomena as depression and lethargy, in the study participants. "Music is one of the best ways to maintain mental acuity, because playing a musical instrument requires simultaneous reading, listening, memorizing, and manual dexterity."

The multi-tasking neurobic benefits associated with making music supports the late-life vitality of rock stars like: Mick Jagger, Keith Richards, Sting, Eric Clapton, Phil Collins, Ozzy Ozbourne, B.B. King, Simon and Garfunkel, and Paul McCartney.

Additionally, boomer rockers are now launching reunion tours in their retirement years: Duran Duran, Motley Crue, and Fleetwood Mac. Jazz pianist, George Shearing released a new album at the age of 85 years. Les Paul was still performing at age eighty-nine; and B.B. King is a national spokesperson in support of healthy lifestyles. Tina Turner continues to rock on stage in her seventh decade.

NEUROBIC WORKOUTS

There are dozens of neurobic exercises that will keep your brain strong and your mind resilient. Here are a few examples.

➤ While driving to work, read a license plate and translate the letters and numbers into a phrase.

➤ Introduce a new scent into your home in the morning. Rather than starting the day by smelling coffee, slice a lemon in half and inhale the aroma.

➤ Change your daily routine. Eat breakfast, then take a shower, or vice versa.

➤ Try eating or brushing your teeth with your left hand if you are right handed, and vice versa.

➤ Go to a new ethnic restaurant, sample new tastes, and make ethnicity the topic of dinner conversation.

If you're among those with a keen sense of intellectual curiosity, you'll find some fine books exploring the science behind the techniques of brain exercise. Check your local public library for the follow titles which are excellent sources for neurobic exercises.

- *Train Your Brain More: 60 days to a better brain* by Kawashima, (2008): daily exercises, based on brain research, for improving and monitoring progress of your brain power.
- *Building Mental Muscle* by Gamon and Bragdon (2003): conditioning exercises for six intelligence zones.
- *Keep Your Brain Alive* by Rubin and Katz (1998): 83 neurobic exercises to help prevent memory loss and increase mental fitness.
- *Building Left-Brain Power* by Bragdon and Gamon (2003): one hundred and four left-brain exercises for building confidence and a positive attitude.
- *Exercises for The Whole Brain* by Bragdon and Gamon (2004): sixty exercises to stimulate brain systems in visual, math, and decision-making skills.
- *The Senior Moments Memory* by Friedman (2010): memory improvement and brain fitness.
- *Brain Power* by Gelb and Howell (2011): how to improve your mind as you age.
- *Use Your Brain to Change Your Age* by Amen (2012): look, think and feel younger every day.

INTELL-AGE-GENCE

The work of Harvard psychologist Dr. Howard Gardner offers a conceptual framework for organizing all the good news into one cognitive map. Gardner, building on the much earlier work of Dr. Alfred Binet (father of the IQ-Intelligence Quotient), has proposed the existence of eight "multiple intelligences" residing in each of us while some are more highly developed than others, the less-used "latent" intelligences carry the potential for further development, "awakening" hidden talents. For more information, you can read Gardner's Intelligence Reframed: Multiple Intelligences for the Twenty-First Century (1999).

Each of Gardner's eight types of intelligence identify a variety of brain powers as demonstrated by the following abilities.

01. **Linguistic intelligence:** commanding use of words to express a variety of thought and emotion.

02. **Logical-mathematical intelligence:** exceptional competency in reasoning out solutions to problems.

03. **Spatial intelligence:** ability to communicate exceptionally well through visual images.

04. **Bodily-kinesthetic intelligence:** physical prowess transforming the body into an instrument of perfect motion.

05. **Musical intelligence:** exceptional ability to capture the essence of organized sound known as rhythm and music.

06. **Interpersonal intelligence:** ability to develop synergy among and between people by orchestrating their ideas.

07. **Intrapersonal intelligence:** ability to transcend oneself from the physical to the metaphysical world.

08. Naturalist intelligence: ability to identify patterns and classify things in nature (plants, animals), as well as sensitivity to other aspects of our natural world (e.g., clouds, rock configurations).

Here's how to build your brain power using what I call *Boomer Brain Boosters* (Demko, 2005), based on Gardner's paradigm. According to Gardner, although we all possess varying degrees of eight intelligences, each individual one intelligence that is the best. We use this one most often used because it is our most powerful intellectual tool.

The Boomer Brain Boosters (below) can help you develop all of your eight intelligences as related to the Youth'n Up Your Life formula for successful aging and active retirement. If you've got eight-cylinders of brain power, why chug along on just one.

BOOMER BRAIN BOOSTERS: the 9 lives of the human brain

The following exercises can be used to tune-up your brain-power engine so that it starts running at its full eight-cylinder potential. Begin by assigning each of the eight Boomer Brain Boosters to a given day of the week.

Linguistic Brain Boosters
- Keep the dictionary handy and learn one new word while sipping your morning cup of coffee.
- Work the daily crossword puzzle in the morning newspaper.

Logical Brain Boosters
- When faced with a problem to solve, immediately reject your first or most obvious solution. That will force your creativity into high gear.
- Learn to say "On the other hand," then offer an alternative explanation. The great philosopher, Baruch Spinoza, said "No matter how thin you slice something, there are still two sides." How would you rephrase Spinoza's quote in your own words?

Spatial Brain Boosters

- Try talking in pictures. For example, your friend asks, "How's things?" Don't speak in words; communicate emotions: "I'm walking on clouds," "I feel like I'm in a rowboat with only one oar."
- Respond to questions by prefacing your answers with "Picture this…" then tell a brief visual "story."

Kinesthetic Brain Boosters

- We all enjoy watching slow motion replays of graceful athletes in action because it gives us an opportunity to witness the style and poise of the athlete's execution.
- Watch your favorite athlete, actor, actress, or other performer. Which of their movements (e.g., walk, a wave to the crowd) do you find most graceful? Practice and model those behaviors.

Musical Brain Boosters

- Try to hum, whistle, or softly sing along with the music in the car, elevator, or wherever you hear music.
- When you can't hum, whistle, or sing, softly drumming your fingers, or tapping your pencil on your coffee cup along with the rhythm of the music around you.

Interpersonal Brain Boosters

- During discussions, play the role of the "strong silent type." Listen to what people are saying. See if you can translate all the ideas into "two sides" of the issue. Then, interject your objective understanding of the issue.
- Take on the role of consensus-builder in social situations. For example, defend both sides of the issue, "I see John's point, but what Martha is saying also rings true." Don't be surprised if people start turning to you more often for your broad-minded opinions.

Intrapersonal Brain Boosters

- Daydream every once in a while. Every great achievement is inspired by dreaming the improbable or impossible. Start with, "If I were President..." or "If I had a million dollars to donate to any cause, I would..." or "If I could live my life all over again, I would...."
- Take five-minute vacations by taking the phone off the hook, closing the office door, and imagine you are in a beautiful vacation spot. This brief respite helps recharge your brain power.

Naturalist Brain Boosters

- Take up bird watching and learn the scientific names and descriptions of the birds in your region.
- Purchase a telescope and learn the names of the planets and constellations, or start a rock collection and explore the various categories and their origins.

The Self-Actualized Mind

- Obviously, if you can "boost" one cylinder of your brain power, then it's possible, at least in theory, to actualize the full potential of your brain power, running on all eight cylinders.
- Borrowing a term from Abraham Maslow's theory of self-actualization, I call the achievement of this "optimal brain power" the *Self-Actualized Mind*.

Here's the point. You possess the potential to expand your brain power in nine dimensions. We all have the same gray matter. So, make sure you put yours to good use.

WHAT IS AND WHAT IS NOT ALZHEIMER'S?

When the topic of conversation turns to age-related memory loss, confusion, and disorientation; Alzheimer's Disease (AD) is the first thing that comes to mind. Decline in cognitive functioning (memory, learning, and thinking) is referred to as "senile dementia." When AD affects personality and mood, it is referred to as "senile psychosis." The same individual can be afflicted with both conditions depending on the location of brain deterioration and the level of progression of the disease. Alzheimer's Disease generally evolves in the following three-stage progression. With the passage of time, which can be ten years, different types of mental power are lost.

Stage One consists of mild, infrequent episodes such as forgetting everyday words, like "Where are the "things" (keys) I need to start the car?"

Stage Two involves increasing disorientation, including getting lost in a familiar setting, requiring continuing support in decision-making, and major intervention and support in the Instrumental Activities of Daily Living (IADL) such as shopping and problem-solving (making judgment calls and decision-making).

Stage Three requires constant attention and complete assistance in the Activities of Daily Learning (ADL) such as eating, dressing, toileting, and anticipating the needs of someone who is no longer capable of thinking, speaking, or doing for themselves.

In addition to AD, there are other origins of cognitive decline. More importantly, these are reversible conditions. For example, any condition that affects the flow of blood, oxygen, and food to the brain cells will result in Acute Brain Syndrome (ABS). Acute refers to a temporary condition that can be reversed, causing the problem behaviors to stop.

These typical sources can lead to acute brain dysfunction (ABS):
- Anemia – reduced red blood cells carry oxygen to brain cells.
- Congestive heart - weakened muscle pumps less blood.
- Low blood pressure - reduced blood volume to the brain.
- Narrowing of carotid artery - reduces blood flow to brain.
- Malnutrition - reduction in supply of nutrients to brain cells.
- Depression - symptoms (memory, confusion) mimic ABS.

Each of these six conditions will respond to medical intervention. So, any suspicion of Alzheimer's disease should first rule out the above causes for problems such as poor judgment, reduced problem-solving skills, short term and long term memory deficits, episodes of disorientation and confusion as to time, place, or person recognition.

The exact origin of Alzheimer's disease is not yet known. As a result, whenever an adult presents questionable symptoms, such as memory loss, it is imperative that health providers first rule-out other less-obvious reasons for cognitive dysfunction, rather than concluding, too quickly, that the condition is Alzheimer's Disease, an as yet irreversible condition.

A FINAL WORD

Your brain responds to exercise at any age. The AMA reports that a one-point increase in cognitive activity can result in a 33 percent decrease in risk to Alzheimer's. A variety of neurobic exercise are readily available to fit every personal style. There's crossword puzzles and chess games that produce impressive results. Also, learning to play a musical instrument, trying out a new language, or just plain learning something new every day are your brain's best friend. Why not try your hand at teaching adults or mentoring young people. Teaching others what you know is one of the ultimate brain boosters. Finally, try reading the rest of this book aloud to yourself and your brain activity will jump at least two-fold.

ZOOMER-FRIENDLY READING – BRAIN BOOSTERS

These resources are in addition to those listed earlier within this chapter pertaining to sources for learning neurobic exercises.

Train Your Brain
Kawashima (2005)

Learning Theories
www.learning-theories.com/gardners-multiple-intelligences-theory.html (2011).

Intelligence Reframed: Multiple Intelligences 21st Century
Gardner (2000).

Multiple Intelligences Around the World: cultural views
Chen, Moran and Gardner (2009).

Use it or Lose it (Arabic Edition)
Bragdon (2008).

Use It or Lose It
Bragdon and Gamon, (2004).

Alzheimer's: research, eldercare, and caregiver support
www.alz.org

Nintendo Puzzle Games
Layton (2011).

Brain Age: Train Your Brain in Minutes a Day
Kawashima (2006).

Ageless Memory: Expert's Rx for a Razor-Sharp Mind
Lorayne (2010).

Brainfit: 10 Minutes a Day for a Sharper Mind and Memory
Gediman and Crinella (2005).

Use Your Brain to Change Your Age
Amen (2012).

6

Physical Fitness: Exercise, Energize, Revitalize

Zoomer fitness regimens combine both aerobics (for energy and endurance) and anaerobics (for strength and flexibility).

B en Franklin was right, "An ounce of prevention is worth more than a pound of cure." It's like ignoring your car's maintenance. Don't change the oil and the engine burns out, the car stops running and you can't drive to work. So now you've lost your job and the bank forecloses on your home. "If only I had spent $200 dollars on prevention, I wouldn't have lost my $200,000 house."

Sure, the example given above seems a gross exaggeration. But its application to healthcare is highly relevant and happens every day. For example, the cost of health care is astronomically expensive, because 75% of illness and disease in America is due to neglect of our bodies, we eat faster than we walk. Change your oil so you won't end up dead before your time.

Fitness is a team sport. Are you "in the game" or "on the bench?" You're "in the game" if you monitor your health risks, then discussing concerns with your doctor, then adopt strategies that lower your risks. Health risks originate from two sources: your parents (genetically-inherited risk-factors) or substandard lifestyle habits. Inherited risks require medical intervention. Lifestyle risks require personal intervention, eliminating daily habits that erode your health and replacing them with habits that promote healthy living.

Pin-pointing the source of a health problem isn't easy, even by your doctor. Neglect one aspect your health, such as failing to get your body weight under control, will likely result in obesity, then obesity may result in loss of muscle mass, decreases the body's ability to perform basic tasks such as lifting the grandkids up, placing groceries into a shopping cart, or rising from a sitting position. As a case in point, a USC research study (journal of Obesity, 2012) found that "the combination of increased weight and decreased muscle mass was much greater than either problem alone." In the USC study, physical problems were 91% higher for obese people who also suffered from low muscle mass.

YOUTH'N UP: PHYSICAL FITNESS QUICK TIPS

Here's what the research says about physical fitness.
- ➤ Morning exercise helps burn more calories all day long.
- ➤ *All prescription medications have side-effects and risks.*
- ➤ High-blood pressure (HBP) must be confirmed by HBP test.
- ➤ *Multiplying body weight (lbs.) by 15 equals daily caloric needs.*
- ➤ Obesity is the most common source of adult-onset diabetes.
- ➤ *NIH.gov offers internet access to 27 health research centers.*
- ➤ Human aging is determined by genetics and lifestyle factors.
- ➤ *Brushing and flossing teeth can reduce the risk of heart disease.*

> ➢ Dividing body weight (lbs) by 2 equals daily water needs in ounces.

Successful aging requires an understanding of both *universal* and *personal* health risks. *Universal health risks* are those common among all mature adults. *Personal health risks* are those based on genetic information inherited from blood relatives: your grandparents, parents, and siblings. For example, the genetic code transferred to you from your parents may very well carry higher than average risks for certain diseases—glaucoma, hypertension, diabetes, cancer—and for certain conditions, such as a tendency toward substance abuse.

Educating yourself about these risks is a relatively simple matter. Free educational materials are available from many credible sources, most notably the National Institutes of Health (NIH). NIH maintains twenty-seven research centers, each focusing on a special area of disease, health care treatment, and prevention. The more you learn about health and wellness, the more you can become an active participant in the doctor-patient partnership.

Partnership means never being afraid to ask questions. Fear or embarrassment can be killers. As far back as 1998, a survey on patient-physician communication issues, conducted by Louis Harris for Pharmacia & Upjohn, found that many patients suffer needlessly due to embarrassment about health problems. Twenty-five percent of patients surveyed admitted that there have been times when they wanted to talk to a doctor about a health problem but were reluctant to do so because of embarrassment.

EMBARRASSED TO DEATH

The Harris survey found embarrassment (25%) is a far more common reason given for avoiding doctor-patient communication. Less common reasons include the following.

Unimportant (11 percent)

"Everyone else in the reception area is worse off than me."

Fear of bad news (8 percent)

"If it's bad news, I just don't care to know."

Don't want to waste doctor's time (8 percent)

"Why bother the doctor with such a minor problem."

Afraid of treatment (7 percent)

"It's going to be painful and it's going to be expensive."

In an earlier study of patient embarrassment, 93 percent of physicians reported serious medical problems could be averted if patients were more willing to talk about their health problems. Two-thirds of the physicians reported difficulties treating patients who were too embarrassed to talk about their problems (Source: Take Time to Talk Advisory Council, 1997).

An opinion poll by AgeVenture News (2006) found sources of embarrassment for male and female retirees included incontinence, erectile dysfunction, uncontrollable flatus, reduced sexual desire, and overactive bladder. In the case of urinary incontinence, "suffering in silence" is unnecessary because of a number of highly effective treatments available; including prescription medication, bladder exercises, and surgery. Doctors believe conquering patients' embarrassment will significantly improve their patients' ability to lead more active, enjoyable lives.

RACE, GENDER AND HEALTH

Race and gender are risk factors, especially in later life. Hispanic women run a higher risk for hypertension. Black women are higher risk for Type-2 diabetes. Caucasian women are higher risk for osteoporosis. Other unique health issues include the high risk for breast cancer and osteoporosis among certain males.

Learn more about minority female health issues at the following online resource: **womenshealth.gov/minority-health**. Health issues related to both male and female minorities and ethnic groups, can be found online at: **erc.msh.org**

Here's the point. Individuals in all ancestral groups should identify and monitor these four areas of health concern:
risks universal to all mature adults,

- risks unique to specific racial groups
- risks unique to gender, and
- risks inherited from blood relatives.

DISEASES CONCURRENT WITH ADVANCING AGE

With the passage of time, your body becomes more vulnerable to wear-and-tear and risk to illness. The leading causes of death among those ages mature adults (listed in descending order) are: heart disease, cancer, stroke, chronic lower respiratory diseases, influenza and pneumonia, diabetes, and bacterial blood poisoning, according to research by the National Institutes of Health (Older Americans 2004: Key Indicators of Well-Being).

Both men and women do not share the same health risks. Men of all races are at higher risk for influenza, pneumonia, diabetes, and accidental injuries. In addition, men are further subject to prostate and testicular cancer. Women of all races are at higher risk for Alzheimer's and kidney diseases. Likewise, based on gender, women are further subject to breast, ovarian, and uterine cancers.

Based on your family health history, you could be either at high-risk, low-risk, or no-risk for certain diseases and conditions. For example, longevity does run in families, as does depression, substance abuse, cancers, hypertension, heart disease, Type 1 diabetes, and Alzheimer's disease.

On the other hand, there is good about your body's ability to resist disease. Middle-aged adults who exercise at least twice a week could reduce their risk of developing Alzheimer's disease by 50 percent (March 2005 study at Stockholm's Gerontology Research Center). "An active lifestyle, physical, mental and social, is preventive," says Stockholm's Mia Kivipelto, PhD, MD, with the Aging Research Center, Karolinska Institute, Stockholm, and the Stockholm Gerontology Research Center.

POLY-PHARMACY: Addiction to Our Medicine Cabinet

There is no doubt that highly developed nations like the United States have become addicted to the medicine cabinet. Rather than suffer through even the most minor pain or temporary pain or discomfort, most Americans opt for a quick-fix. "Take a pill."

According to The Prescription and Over-the-Counter Drug Guide for Seniors (2004), "People over the age of 65 represent 14 percent of the U.S. population but consume more than one-third of prescription medications. The average senior citizen uses more than five different medications each day, not counting nonprescription, over-the-counter drugs, and herbals or vitamins, which as many as 90 percent of seniors take." Don't always expect your appointment to result in a prescription for yet another medication. If it's called for, then you should have it. But, too many adults are addicted to their medicine cabinet, thinking that the path to health is built solely on medication. The trend of drug companies' direct marketing to consumers has worsened this situation. Listen closely to both the sales pitch and the drug side-effect warnings. Sometimes the consumer is trading one problem for another.

We have a drug for everything. So, why not an age prevention drug? There has been a perpetual search for an "anti-aging" pill ever since Ponce de Leon pursued the proverbial Fountain of Youth. Why actively engage in health maintenance when we can just sit around and wait for science to tell us wait what new "pill to pop?" Besides, doctors, like everyone else, can make mistakes.

In the February 2005 issue of the Journal of the American Geriatrics Society, researchers reported that 28 percent of mature consumers were prescribed medications deemed potentially inappropriate by medical experts, while 5 percent received a drug that had been classified as inappropriate in all older patients. The federal government estimates that 250,000 adults receive the wrong medication each year at a cost of $4 billion.

We do have a choice. You can pop pills in order to quell your "age-aches." Or, you can take a proactive route. Learn the source of your symptoms, then adopt the health maintenance lifestyle strategies known to ameliorate many of those age-aches.

A prevention initiative, launched by BlueCross/BlueShield Association in early 2005 provided consumers with a brown bag to bring all their prescriptions, over-the-counter drugs, and dietary supplements to their doctors' offices for review. Subsequently, 33 percent of those consumers received prescription changes, 64 percent had medications added, 47 percent had some prescriptions stopped, and 65 percent had dosages changed. Drugs are too costly to make such mistakes. In 2007, AARP reported that prices of brand name drugs increased at two to three times the rate of inflation.

The moral of this story is "two heads are better than one." You and your doctor need to work as a team, promoting your health and well-being. Hey, even the Lone Ranger didn't work alone. He had Tonto and Trigger.

CHECKING UNDER THE HOOD: Health Wise

Assessment of your health status should include:

- annual physical exam, age-specific vaccinations i.e. shingles,
- annual eye exam (prescription check and glaucoma test),
- annual podiatric exam and footwear prescription, if needed
- six-month dental inspection and cleaning,
- bi-annual review of nutrition and dietary status.

These checkups are increasingly important with each passing year.

Your annual physical exam is important because many of the diseases of adulthood, such as hypertension and certain cancers, occur without symptoms. The only way to tell for sure if you are a candidate for these diseases is to get checked. Your healthcare provider can devise a comprehensive exam based on your age, gender, race, and family health history. Remember, your health risks are unique. Get to know your health provider very well, and you will most likely stay well.

Your annual eye exam is important for detection of cataracts, glaucoma, macular degeneration, and other age-related eye diseases that may be preventable if diagnosed early. The American Academy of Ophthalmology recommends the following comprehensive eye exams schedule for adults: twice between the ages of thirty and thirty-nine; every two to four years between the ages of forty and sixty-four; every one or two years after age sixty-five. Given the high risk of asymptomatic diseases such as glaucoma (especially in African Americans) and macular degeneration in the entire older population, these examinations are prudent.

Your foot and footwear exam are fundamental for maintaining an active lifestyle. In-grown nails, toe injuries, diabetes and ill-fitted shoes cause discomfort can cause you to avoid walking which also results in decreased exercise and lower energy level. "The journey of a 1,000 miles begins with the first step" (Chinese proverb). If you can't make that first step, you aren't going anywhere.

Your dental inspection and teeth cleaning offers protection against the risks of oral cancer, gum disease, tooth decay, and the possible spread of inflammation from infected gums. Again, early detection is the key. Get checked every six months. Do not wait until a problem surfaces.

Your nutrition and dietary reviews have become increasingly popular as adults rediscover the time-worn health adage, "You are what you eat." Be sure to consult qualified sources offered by a state-licensed professional. For example, the title "nutritionist" offers no guarantee of expertise because that title is not regulated like the "registered dietician" who is professionally trained and licensed to provide advice on nutrition, diet, food, and dietary supplements.

A VERB ABOUT VITAMINS: "CAUTION"

Vitamins and minerals are excellent tools for reducing health risks. But, if you "eat your veggies" and follow sound dietary advice, you may not need to rely on supplements. When it comes to nutrition, there's nothing like the real thing—fresh fruits and vegetables, and whole grains.

If you do use dietary supplements (prescription or over-the-counter), let your doctor know what you are taking. Taking fewer vitamins is often better than taking an excess of vitamins. A consultation with a registered dietician is a good backup plan because, despite their medical school training, physicians are no match for registered dieticians who have substantial training in nutrition and dietary needs.

While there are many exotic, mega-vitamin products available, the best you'll find are the daily supplement variety providing FDA-recommended dosages of vitamins and minerals. These include the once-a-day, all-in-one, tablets sold under well-known, tried-and-true corporate names where there is evidence of clinical trials supporting product claims. Well-known companies have a lot to lose financially and in reputation if their product harms the consumer. For mature adults, there are special editions of vitamins based on men's and women's needs.

Don't forget to educate yourself so you can be an active partner in health maintenance. The practice of medicine has never been more complex. The year I was graduated from the University of Michigan (1982), the school found it necessary to create a new doctoral program in "consulting pharmacist" which was created to provide doctors with a University-trained expert on prescription medications.

Up until 1982, the sole source of pharmaceutical information came primarily from the salesmen employed by the drug companies. Not exactly an unbiased source of pharmaceutical advice.

THE LAST WORD ON LASTING LONGER

Human lifespan, according to science is 120 years. However, today's life-expectancy falls four decades short, 80 years. Can you get back any of those "lost" forty years? Yes. In fact, the CDC predicts one million boomers will live to be 100 years of age. You can improve your odds of living 20 years longer than most people. Here's how. Eat healthy, exercise, avoid drug abuse, use alcohol in moderation, monitor your health risks and do not smoke. The health risks from smoking (cigarettes, pipes, cigars) include lung cancer, oral and throat cancer, and heart disease.

Log-on to Medline, a web site service of the U.S. National Library of Medicine and the National Institutes of Health. This internet resource provides consumers with science-based information on 650 health topics, conditions, and diseases. You will also find a Medical Encyclopedia of "A to Z" information on health and medicine. Use the web site's calculator to determine your risk of having a heart attack within the next ten years, just in time to adopt strategies that will reduce your risk. Medline's address is: http://hin.nhlbi.nih.gov

A FINAL WORD

Promote personal wellness by practicing prevention. **First,** if you are in good health, maintain it. **Second,** focus on prevention by learning the health risks unique to your age group, gender, ethnicity, and genetic inheritance (family health history). **Third,** monitor your health risks through regular check-ups. **Four,** share what you have learned with family and friends.

ZOOMER-FRIENDLY READING – PHYSICAL FITNESS

Top Screw-ups Doctors Make and How to Avoid Them
Graedon and Graedon (2011).

Medline's Medical Encyclopedia
medlineplus.gov/

Resources for older visually impaired
www.acb.org/resources/older.html

Exercise and Physical Fitness: MedlinePlus
www.nlm.nih.gov/exerciseandphysicalfitness.html

Calculate your risk of heart attack
www.nhlbi.nih.gov/actintime/rhar/rhar.htm

National Academy of Sports Medicine
http://www.nasm.org/

President's Council on Sports, Fitness and Nutrition
http://fitness.gov

7

Social Fitness: Grow Your Social Network

Zoomers orchestrate a social support system of companions, close friends, and a confidante.

"People who need people are the luckiest people in the world," according to vocal diva, Barbara Streisand. Science agrees. Social interaction keeps your mental powers sharp. The lack of positive human interaction changes your brain chemistry in a way that severely reduces your decision-making and problem-solving skills (Social Neuroscience, November 2006).

Behavioral research confirms that social acceptance is "absolutely fundamental to humans" (Current Directions in Psychological Science, 2011; 20). Think about it. Why are Reality TV shows so compelling? The episodes focus on individuals who are either "accepted" or "rejected" by the group. This "accept-reject" theme also applies to

TV Soap Operas. That's why grandma insists on watching "my story" where characters are accepted, then rejected, then accepted once more ... until the next episode. You better tune-in tomorrow and find out. Internet dating services are just the same. Will you be accepted or rejected? The human drama is captivating and continuous.

It's time to abandon your vicarious lifestyle. Get off the bench and into the game. Today's adventurous seniors sky-dive at age seventy-nine, climb Mount Fuji at age eighty-four, and bungee jump at ninety-three years of age.

Setting new goals is like creating a new future. It taking our focus off of daily aches, pains and boring routines. New goals re-direct our thoughts and actions toward the world around us. It stretches our reach beyond our grasp. It leads to self-pride and the admiration of significant others. Life will feel good again.

YOUTH'N UP: SOCIAL FITNESS QUICK TIPS

Here's what the research says about growing your social network.

➢ Couples live five years longer than those who live alone.
➢ Socializing and spending time alone are equally important.
➢ Voluntary service increases life-expectancy by two years.
➢ Living alone shortens life-expectancy, unless you own a pet.
➢ Laughter improves your brain chemistry just like aerobics.
➢ Sexual promiscuity reduces life-expectancy by six years.
➢ Couples who share household chores report higher levels of life satisfaction.
➢ Travel programs now incorporate opportunities for both education and voluntary service.

Continued social interaction is fundamental for achieving a "sense of purpose" in life. Everyone needs a reason to get up, dressed, and out every day. It's a fact, meaningful lives last longer, and are lived with a greater sense of fulfillment and joy.

Self-employed people often never retire, preferring to pursue their chosen profession and passion. Each year, during the month of May,

Older Americans Month, the nation celebrates the careers of older workers still on the job in the ninth and tenth decade of life. Employment isn't the only option for a meaningful life. Voluntary service, political office, education, travel, leisure, and writing are among the many lifestyles currently pursued by adults who continue to be intellectually curious about their world, and courageous in their pursuit of life-long goals.

MY STORY

My days are filled with providing college instruction, public speeches, guest spots on talk-radio and television, research, writing, interviews by magazines and newspapers, and editing of a syndicated news service. Like you, my days are full. But, it doesn't seem like work because I love what I do.

What remains a mystery to me is how I got to this point of relative success. My early years were full of self-doubt, insecurity, and disabling shyness.

It all started when my first grade teacher assigned each student to read aloud from a book. After listening to each student's oration, the teacher assigned us to reading groups based upon level of reading comprehension. Most of my classmates read well enough to be assigned to reading groups called "Airplane Class" or "Car Class." My miserable classroom reading performance earned me a spot in the third reading group called "Wagon Class." There I was at the tender age of six; my fate sealed. Branded as "Wagon Class Dave."

The remainder of my life, up through four years of college, consisted of no courage to ask anyone for a date, failing three attempts at speech class, and literally dying a thousand deaths during my first, second, and third public speeches.

My past doesn't matter much now because I believe both success and failure provide an opportunity to learn something about yourself and grow from each experience. I did it; rising from the "Wagon Class" to achieve self-confidence, happiness and financial success. Not bad for a "Wagon Class" guy.

A NEW BEGINNING

Youth represents self-confidence, a sense of style, and a healthy connection with the world. "Time and the river" can cause individuals to disengage, drift away from the mainstream of life, and disconnect from the world, perhaps abandon any hope of a brighter future. This chapter focuses on social fitness—developing and strengthening our sense of self in order to engage our world in ways that really matter, to us and to others.

Read on, and discover ways to live life to the fullest whether for fun, profit, or anything in-between, such as employment, second career, education, voluntary service, action adventure, tourism, and cultivating a social network of diverse friendships.

Youth'n Up Your Life: Super Self-Image

Self-image is a combination of self-concept (the roles you play in life) and self-esteem (how well you perform your roles). It's possible, then to improve your self-image in one of two ways. Increase the number of roles you play by taking on new responsibilities, or improving your competency in your current roles. There's also a third way to improve self-image. Do both. Add roles and increase your role competency.

Youth preservation depends on building your self-concept (repertoire of roles), and boosting role competency by self-instruction, formal education or enlisting a seasoned mentor (published author, personal coach). Playing a positive role (work, parent, volunteer, and friend) improves self-concept. Performing those roles in a competent manner generates positive feedback, which improves self-esteem. Here's the point. Humans perform a balancing act between taking-on new roles (sometimes while exiting old roles) and learning to be competent in those roles.

Youth'n Up from the INSIDE Out

"We are what we share." We can share our time and talents. What gift (talent) inside you is waiting to be shared? That's your Inside waiting to get Out. Here's an example. Forced retirement results in transition from a socially valued (you get paid) to the ambiguous status of "retiree." The term "retiree" explains where you have been, but not where you are going. Time to set sail for life's next adventure. What do you have to offer the world?

Medical research documents the significant role played by our self-image. Self-image refers to how we answer questions that go to the very core of our identity and self-worth. Who are you? What is it that you have to share? When are you headed?

As far back as the mid-1970s, the National Institute of Mental Health (NIMH) underscored the importance of self-image. NIMH stated that "The average life expectancy of a white-collar male (at retirement age 65) is only 36 to 40 months." Retirement has become a socially manufactured death sentence. Depending on how an individual copes with this transition, life-expectancy could increase or decrease. Who are you? Where are you headed?

Many adults manage to avoid this "retirement crisis." They have overcome the challenges to their self-image by redirecting their lives toward meaningful roles. The result? These re-directed adults enjoy a life expectancy increase of more than fifteen to eighteen years.

The energy and strength necessary for increasing our self-image comes from within. But, the opportunity for personal growth doesn't stop there. Energy and strength is also drawn from our relationships with significant others, personal growth fostered from the outside and drawn in to ourselves.

Youth'n Up from the OUTSIDE In

The features we associate with the idea of "being human" are not just the product of genetic inheritance. To a very large part, our human qualities are learned through interaction with others, a process called socialization. Developmental psychology long ago confirmed the process of socialization as an absolutely essential factor in normal growth and development. We draw energy and inspiration through our interactions with family, co-workers, companions, friends, and confidantes. Socialization offers us a continuum of opportunities for personal growth.

First, there's socializing for the purpose of companionship, for mutual benefit while pursuing a common goal. Examples include shared travel, volunteer service, team projects, shared housing, and shared supportive care.

Second, there's socializing for the purpose of friendship, what we call emotionally-charged socialization. Examples include sharing time in joyous action or reflective silence, sharing news of common interest, and daring to speak our thoughts out loud.

Third, there's socializing for the purpose of intimacy, being with a soul mate who listens empathetically to our high hopes or low moods. Intimacy does not adhere to a fixed schedule. Whether for romance or crisis, a confidante other is there for us whenever the need arises, no matter what time or circumstance.

The benefits of a well-rounded social life are well-documented. The National Institute of Mental Health predicts that a major benefit of having a confidante (a soul mate who shares your joys and comforts your sorrows) is an increase in life expectancy by at least two years.

Remember, you can't find that "someone special" until you find yourself. Start exploring the new roles outlined earlier to discover your interests and strengths.

- Like to learn? Enroll in a course or workshop.
- Enjoy cultural experiences? Take an expert-guided tour.
- Feel good fulfilling needs? Sign-up to volunteer.

Your new experiences can transform you into a great storyteller capable of entertaining and inspiring others.

WE ARE WHAT WE SHARE

The opportunities for engaging the world are as numerous as the talents you have to offer. Review the dozens of ways to express your talents and gifts through roles in advocacy, adventure, education, employment, and voluntary service.

Make a Difference: Be an Advocate

National Council on the Aging: www.ncoa.org
- Provides opportunities for conferences, learning, and volunteering in support of fulfilling the needs of the older

population. NCOA creates public-private partnerships, and raises public awareness of aging issues.

- *American Association of Retired Persons* (AARP): www.aarp.org
- Learn about new policies and programs impacting seniors on all aspects of retirement. AARP offers free tax help for seniors, maintains a speaker's bureau, and brings people together online to discuss living on Social Security.

Over the Hill and Back to School

This decade, college campuses experienced a twenty percent increase in students aged 40 to 64 years (U.S. News and World Report, 2007). You might also want to experience the world firsthand, beyond textbooks and lectures. Here are just a few examples of experiential learning opportunities.

- *Boom-Boom Cards*

When you travel the world, why just collect souvenirs when you can create treasured memories. BoomBoomCards.com is an Internet web site that collects cards from people all over the world. The cards describe community needs in many geographical regions where you can go and work alongside the locals on voluntary service projects. It's a kind of "Pay It Forward" (giving back) experience. Many such programs are now available from a variety of vendors, so be sure to background-check before you sign-up or pay fees.

- *Road Scholars*: www.roadscholar.org

Road Scholar offers "adventures in lifelong learning" with a twist. There's walking, hiking and biking through national parks with a tour guide who serves as an expert on local points of interest.

- *Elderhostel*: www.elderhostel.org
- Want the world to be your classroom? Elderhostel offers over 10,000 programs a year in ninety countries. It is one of the world's largest educational and travel organization exclusively for senior adults.
- *Global Volunteers*: www.globalvolunteers.org
- "Learn first-hand about your host community's culture and history while gaining new perspectives of the world during one, two, or three weeks."

Voluntary Service

- *Senior Core of Retired Executives* (SCORE): www.score.org
- Use your experience and expertise to help grow small businesses.
- *Foster Grandparent Program*

"The Foster Grandparent Program provides a way for those 60 and over, whose incomes are limited, to serve as extended family members to children and youth with exceptional needs. Foster grandparents serve 20 hours a week in schools, hospitals, correctional institutions, daycare facilities, and Head Start centers."

- *Senior Companion Program*

"The Senior Companion Program provides a way for those 60 and over, whose incomes are limited, to provide assistance and friendship to adults who have difficulty with daily living tasks, such as grocery shopping and bill paying. Senior Companions spend 20 hours a week helping an average of two to four adult clients live independently in their own homes.

- *Retired Senior Volunteer Program*: www.seniorcorps.org/

Volunteers "serve in a diverse range of nonprofit organizations, public agencies, and faith-based groups. They mentor at-risk youth, organize neighborhood watch programs, test drinking water for contaminants, teach English to immigrants, and lend their business skills to community groups that provide critical social services."

- *Habitat for Humanity*: www.habitat.org

"This is a Christian organization that helps build affordable houses for those in need. Now at work in one hundred countries, Habitat is building a house every twenty-six minutes."

- *Peace Corps*: www.peacecorps.gov

Not just for college students anymore, the Peace Corps offers you the opportunity to make a lasting difference in someone's life. Today's volunteers are teachers, agricultural workers, information technology specialists, business consultants, environmentalists and health professionals.

Employment and Careers

U.S. Chamber of Commerce: www.uschamber.com
The Chamber of Commerce provides information about small businesses and job opportunities.

- *Association for Gerontology in Higher Education*: www.aghe.org
Promotes gerontology as a career choice, and educates communities about the processes of aging and the implications of an aging society.

- *Experience Works*: www.experienceworks.org
A national, nonprofit organization providing training and employment services for mature workers. The organization reaches over 125,000 mature adults annually in 50 states and Puerto Rico."
Remember how this chapter began? Youth represents confidence, style, and a healthy connection to your social world. Becoming "old" is often described as becoming increasingly disconnected from the world around us. Stay connected. Follow these three steps on a journey back to the real world.

1. Visit your local bookstore and review the new nonfiction publications on lifestyle and fashion. Don't forget the magazine rack.
2. Visit DVD movie and CD music stores. Browse "new release" displays. You don't have to like what you hear and see. But you should be aware of what's popular.
3. Make a point of fostering new relationships with people outside your age group. Volunteering is one way to interface with the younger generation. Part-time work is another. Talking to people with different perspectives on life can be a refreshing way to stimulate your thinking, and help you become more conversant with younger people. Make a point to smile more often, and offer a friendly greeting to those you encounter. Making feel valued can boost your spirits.

A FINAL WORD

You don't have to deny your age, but you don't have to let it define you either. Stop counting years, and start counting the number of new things you want to learn, new places you want to go, and new people you want to meet. Youth'n up your life in every way you can.

ZOOMER FRIENDLY READING – SOCIAL FITNESS

The Boomer's Guide to the New Work Place
Fein (2006).

The Right Questions: for an Extraordinary Life
Ford (2004).

How to Care for Aging Parents
Morris (2004).

Intimacy Factor: Ground Rules for Overcoming Obstacles
Mellody (2004).

It's Never Too Late to Plant a Tree: 65 Inspiring Stories
Helitzer and Helitzer (2003).

The Grown-Up Girl's Guide to Style
Schwab (2006).

Forever Cool: Achieve Ageless Style
Mathieson (2007).

How Not to Look Old: Ways to Look 10 Years Younger
Krupp (2008).

Frumpy to Foxy in 15 Minutes Flat
Rubin and Mauceri (2005).

Frumpy to Fabulous
Jobity (2011).

The Style Checklist: Ultimate Wardrobe Essentials
Boston (2010).

For Men Only: Guide to the Inner Lives of Women
Feldhahn and Feldhahn (2006).

Mars and Venus on a Date: 5 Stages of Dating
Gray (2009).

The Tao of Dating
Binazir (2010).

8

Identity Fitness: An Ageventurous Life

Zoomers enjoy a positive self-concept, self-effacing sense of humor and a passion for living life to the fullest.

Time to spread your wings and fly...rediscover the new you. It's never too late. At age of 65, life expectancy can actually increase nearly two decades. With all that time on your hands, where are you headed? Explore opportunities to experience people and places that will expand your horizons and broaden your perspective on life. "Every face is strange, when you're a stranger" (Jim Morrison, The Doors). What you are likely to discover is a whole new you.

YOUTH'N UP: IDENTITY FITNESS QUICK TIPS

➢ Mature travelers log over 180 million trips per year.
➢ Experience cultures first-hand and mingle with the locals.
➢ Travel motivates you to learn new languages.
➢ Investigate tour-and-volunteer programs *before* you sign-on.
➢ Use a Certified Travel Agent to plan your travel.
➢ Schedule a two-day, post-vacation rest period.
➢ Take half the luggage and twice the spending money.

VACATION STEP 1 of 4: Why People Travel

Not sure where to go? Learn from experience. Some people enjoy a passive, observational tour of the countryside. But that's just half the story. On the other hand, the more adventurous traveler wants an up-close-and-personal adventure, a chance to smell the roses and plant them too.

A survey by Grand Circle Travel identified what most adults want for their travel dollar: experience cultures first hand and meet local residents (43 percent), expert tour guides who know the region, (17 percent), plenty of time to fully explore each travel site (15 percent), enjoy worry-free experiences (8 percent), and socializing with fellow travelers (8 percent).

When it came to pet peeves, airline travel (including delays and overcrowding) was the biggest headache. That's a topic to which frequent travelers can relate!

VACATION STEP 2 of 4: Leave Expert Decisions to Experts

In today's complex travel market, you need an expert to guide you through all the so-called bargains, discounts, and web sites. The Institute of Certified Travel Agents (ICTA) grants the CTC certification to travel professionals who have attained at least five years of full-time travel industry experience, have completed a rigorous academic study program and examination, and follow a continuing education regimen to remain current on the latest travel trends.

When shopping for a travel agent, ask if that agent is professionally certified. Many agents display their certificate in their offices or print this information on their business cards, web sites, and Yellow Page advertisements. In its efforts to establish standards of excellence in the travel industry, the ICTA offers a variety of educational resources (listed below). So, when you need expert advice, make sure you get it from a genuine expert.

VACATION STEP 3 of 4: Preparation

Medical researchers at Prudential Healthcare released the following checklist to ZOOMER magazine (ZoomerBoomerMagazine.com) for those who want to prevent health hazards that might disrupt or cut short your travel plans.

Things to take with you - medication and prescriptions, emergency contact numbers, exercise clothing, eyeglass prescriptions, sunscreen for all climates, glare-reduction sunglasses. Before leaving home, make sure your healthcare coverage is portable; use luggage with wheels; don't over-pack luggage.

Warm weather tips - use sunscreen on exposed areas; bring lightweight, long-sleeved attire and a hat; drink plenty of water (thirst-quenching colas will not hydrate your bod); bring after-swim eardrops if you plan on taking a dip.

Cold weather tips - layer clothing and wear a hat; drink plenty of water, use sunscreen on exposed areas.

On the airplane - try to walk around the cabin every half hour (but observe the seatbelt signs) and drink plenty of water to prevent dehydration—the longer the flight, the more need for water and walking.

VACATION STEP 4 of 4: Pre-Vacation Rest & Relaxation

Fifty-four percent of the Americans return from vacation more tired than before they left, including 19 percent who say they returned feeling "very tired" or "exhausted" (Gallup Survey). Poor planning, later bedtimes, and uncomfortable accommodations were cited as the main reasons for post-trip fatigue.

Here's what these experts advise:

Start packing several days before you leave. Select, fold, and put clothes aside if you worry about wrinkles. Don't wait until the night before.

Don't over-extend yourself before vacation. Get several consecutive good nights of sleep before leaving. If you regularly have trouble falling asleep or staying asleep, see your doctor.

Stay comfortable. Pack your favorite pajamas. If there's room in your suitcase, pack your pillow. Ask the reservation desk to put you in a room away from the elevator, ice machine, or busy street.

Eat and drink moderately. Overeating affects sleep by causing indigestion. Alcohol consumption may cause you to awaken during the night.

Plan to get a full night's sleep. Vacation is supposed to be rejuvenating. You won't sleep if you approach vacation like a marathon.

Stop worrying. Don't put work, family, or financial problems on the itinerary. If you must work during vacation, limit your efforts only to high-priority tasks.

TRAVEL PROFILES FOR EVERY PERSONALITY

Now that you're prepared for travel, what are you waiting for? Time to select a destination and a theme for your travel adventure. What follows is a list of themes (travel profiles) from which to choose depending upon the type of experience that fits your personality.

TRAVEL PROFILE: Fun in the Sun

There's something for everyone in the United States Virgin Islands (USVI): St. John, St. Thomas, and St. Croix. These destinations vacations offer relaxation designed to rejuvenate your body, mind and spirit. As a protectorate of the United States, the USVI allows you to get away without many of the inconveniences associated with getting away. It's as easy as 1-2-3. First, the USVI is an English-speaking destination, so there's no need to bone up on language skills. Second, the currency is in U.S. dollars, so there's no need to worry about exchange rates. Third, as a U.S. territory, no passport is required. You do, however, need evidence of U.S. citizenship.

1. Adventure travelers will enjoy the thrill of kayaking, horseback riding, hiking, snorkeling, parasailing, scuba diving, and casino gambling. St. Thomas and St. Croix also offer some of the best golf greens in the Caribbean.

2. Cultural and historical buffs will find countless museums, sugar mills, rum factories, and centuries-old houses of worship to explore.
   Don't miss the live jazz, Caribbean bands, and riveting theatrical performances.

3. Shop-till-you-drop vacationers will find every kind of quaint boutique imaginable. And there's a generous duty-free shopping allowance that rivals any other Caribbean destination.

4. Eco-tourists will delight in the abundance of wildlife sanctuaries, nature walks through a tropical rain forest, a living desert, and underwater snorkel trails. St. Croix offers a living desert on its north shore and a rain forest at the south end. Be sure to schedule a visit with the beer-drinking hogs. Toss a full can their way and the hogs catch it in their teeth, suck out the beer, then spit out the can. Don't miss it.

5. Gourmet diners will enjoy multi-cultural variety of foods, including samplings of the West Indian delights: kallaloo, johnny cakes, fungi, and fresh seafood galore. Enjoy these island treats with a tall glass of maubi, the favorite local beverage.

6. Newlyweds and couples will find romantic getaways, secluded beaches, cozy bed-and-breakfast inns, and exotic resorts. Celebs and movie stars frequent the island resorts.

7. Grandparents with grandkids will find plenty of "soft-adventure" activities with special rates. A great way to share time and create memories with loved ones.

TRAVEL PROFILE: Searching for Fountains of Youth

As an East-West crossroads, Hong Kong is the perfect place to learn, first-hand, how Chinese people battle stress and fatigue, valuable skills in today's fast-paced world. The Chinese have been unraveling the mysteries of longevity for centuries. The ingredients for a long life are Chinese medicine, healthy dining, herbal tea, Qigong, Tai Chi, and acu-points massage.

Chinese medicine: According to local legion, all of life involves the balancing of opposing forces (Yin and Yang). When balance is disturbed in our bodies, our health suffers. To correct the imbalance, an herbalist will prescribe a variety of roots, barks, twigs, seeds, and flowers. Take a stroll through Hong Kong's Nam Pak Hong, the center of the city's wholesale ginseng and medicinal-herb trade.

Healthy dining: For the Chinese, eating and health can never be separated. They eat to keep healthy and live long. Winter diets include exotic ingredients to keep warm and preserve energy. Every food item, from bamboo shoots to bananas to ginger, has its known properties of heating or cooling, balancing the body's natural forces. Visitors to Hong Kong often visit a specialty tonic restaurant to enjoy a "tonic lunch" prepared with a variety of herbal ingredients.

Herbal tea: The art of tea drinking is quintessentially Chinese. Tea is drunk for health, and is poured as an offering to friends. It accompanies an everyday dim sum breakfast. The best way to learn about the many facets of this Chinese practice is to visit specialty tea shops to learn the technique of proper tea brewing.

Qigong: Qi is the life force. It flows through everything, say the Chinese. And you can control your Qi by engaging in *Qigong* which is an ancient form of exercise allowing one to direct the flow of life force which restores health and improves fitness. Learn the basics of channeling Qi from a *Qigong* master who will demonstrate breathing exercises to cleanse the body and improve circulation.

Tai Chi: Every morning at sunrise, thousands of Hong Kong residents head for the tranquil parks, beaches, and rolling hills to practice the ancient art of Tai Chi, also known as Chinese Shadow boxing. This slow-motion ballet consists of gentle exercise through selected movements learned from a Tai Chi master. After working up an appetite, residents take a refreshing break of tea with dim sum.

Acu-points massage: Where did acupuncture originate? No one knows for sure. Centuries of trial and error evolved into a refined and detailed massage. The Chinese believe that adding pressure to certain points on the body enhances the circulation. In Hong Kong, acu-point massage is as common a remedy as aspirin for aches and pains.

TRAVEL PROFILE: Domestic Action-Adventure

For Brave Hearts, National Geographic Adventure magazine selects and ranks trips. Here are the most popular action adventures.

- Rafting the Colorado River in the Grand Canyon of Arizona.
- Sea Kayaking in the Na Pali Coast in Kauai, Hawaii.
- Dog sledding in the Brooks Range, Alaska.

Log-on to the National Geographic web site where you will find adventure travel details and links to live-action on television and YouTube at: www.natgeomagazines.com

A FINAL WORD

Some people spend so much time trying to improve their life, there's no time left to enjoy it. If you have not already begun, start to explore the planet. Your most important discovery just might be a *whole new you.*

ZOOMER-FRIENDLY READING:
ACTION-ADVENTURE

A major decision confronts every vacation traveler. "Where do I go?" Your travel destination options are as wide-ranging as you can imagine. Problem is, today's whirlwind lifestyles don't allow much time to imagine all the options. Does this sound all too familiar? "If this is Thursday, then Mary goes to soccer practice, Bobby goes to piano lessons, and it's taco-night for dinner… and I've got to find time to finish that report that is due tomorrow."

The following resources are a good place to start learning about plans and themes associated with travel adventure.

1,000 Places to See Before You Die

Workman Publishing (2003).
Author, Patricia Schultz offers travelers a "divide and conquer" strategy for imagining one-thousand travel options. The globe is subdivided into geographic regions, each focusing on exceptional destinations.

Details about each destination appear in capsule summaries readers can digest in a minute or two. Want to stay close to home? Check out a copy of the second book, *1,000 Places to See Before You Die* – USA and Canada edition.

Rick Steves' Easy Access Europe

Guide for Travelers with Limited Mobility (2006).
This guide addresses accessibility issues at the world's top travel destination, Europe. Identifies special needs of slow walkers and wheelchair users. With the help of accessibility organizations in each locale, the author deleted sights, activities, hotels, and restaurants that aren't accessible to the mobility challenged. Readers will also find information about local lodges with a heart for those needing a little extra accessibility help. For all travelers, see *Rick Steves' Europe Through the Back Door* (2011).

Gene Kilgore's Ranch Vacations
Avalon Travel Publishing (2005).
"Number 1 for ranch vacations" is how adventure travelers rate this guidebook, now in its seventh edition. No wonder. Gene Kilgore's book offers a comprehensive scope, meticulous detail, authoritative advice, and full-color illustrations. Readers will find ranch vacation destinations in eleven of the United States and Canada. The author provides a list of questions that travelers should ask prior to making reservations.

- Does the resort have a children's program?
- Do you have off-season rates?
- Will the resort cater to special diets?
- What equipment is provided, and what must I bring?
- What policies do you have for smoking, liquor, cell phones?
- Do you provide transportation to and from the airport?

Europe by Eurail
Touring Europe by Train, (2011).
The authors report on train fares, schedules, and pass options, as well as detailed information on more than ninety specific rail excursions.

Trips start from any of 21 cities with details about historic cities, romantic villages, and scenic hamlets. Readers will find sample rail-tour itineraries on day excursions and fifteen-day rail-tour packages.

CDC Health Information for International Travel 2012
This CDC "Yellow Book" is named for its traditionally yellow cover and is officially titled Health Information for International Travel, serves as authoritative guide for vital pre-travel healthcare recommendations and information about health risks abroad.

GlobeAware.org
"Finding volunteer trips that actually help" reported by Marnie Hunter, CNN, June 2010.

www.GoodIntents.org
How to evaluate volunteer opportunities abroad.

9

Spiritual Fitness: Connect To A Higher Power

Zoomers create a broad repertoire of coping skills that incorporate the undeniable strengths of science and faith.

Those who practice their religion enjoy longer life and better health. Spirituality has also been found to be a significant factor in the healing and recovery process (Religion and Health Research at Duke University, Koenig, 2007). This chapter explores the many life- enhancing applications of the metaphysical world of spirituality.

SPIRITUAL FITNESS QUICK TIPS

➢ Faith has been found to be an immune system booster based on the study of seniors living in high-risk environments.

➢ 95 percent of Americans believe in God as creator and overseer of evolution (Gallup Polls).

➢ Humans are genetically predisposed to believe in God (Dr. Dean Hamer, geneticist, National Institutes of Health).

➢ 40 percent of American scientists subscribe to the notion that God guides evolution.

➢ Prayer significantly aids survival rate of heart surgery patients (Dartmouth Medical School).

➢ Time spent in private devotion positively affects personal health (Duke University).

➢ Religious involvement offers a coping mechanism for elders under stress (University of California-Berkeley).

➢ Spiritual grandparents are healthier and more involved with grandkids (Penn State Univ of North Carolina).

➢ Charles Darwin argued in support of intelligent design in addition to his theory of evolution.

THE GENESIS OF TRANSCENDENCE

What is the meaning of life? As the Boomers enter later-life (metaphorically singing "Nearer My God to Thee"), more and more attention and news coverage is given to religious inquiry. All this attention to God tends to ruffle the feathers of the scientific community. This debate between science and religion will most likely never be resolved. Science is based on empirical evidence, not faith. Religion is based on faith, not empirical evidence.

Whether your interpretation of mankind's purpose is grounded in science or faith, you still believe in something bigger than yourself. Faith in a higher power, as seen in Alcoholics Anonymous.

HEAVEN KNOWS WE WANT TO KNOW

What we all seem to have in common is a need to understand, to make sense of our world. Knowing makes allows us to feel self-efficacy which is a sense that we are in control of our life choices and events.

For example, a seemingly inexplicable event occurs and we don't know the cause. So, we make up plausible scenarios. Your professor fails to show up at the beginning of class. Where is he? Well, if there are 40 students in class, there will be 40 different reasons why everyone thinks the professor is late: he's sick, had an accident, still asleep in his office? Knowledge is power. It makes helps us feel secure, in control.

MATURE TRANSCENDENCE

Gerontologists explain that with increasing age, we become less of a physical being and more of a spiritual being. What is the significance of our life? Time seems to be passing much more quickly as we age. It's easy to understand why. One year to a four year old equal 25% of his life experience, so time seems to move very slow. That same year to an eighty year old is a mere fraction ($1/80^{th}$) of his life. .is Dr. Robert Butler in "Mental Health and Aging" referred to this phenomenon as "transcendence of self."

Likewise, the early work of gerontologist Bernice Neugarten explained the event of "taking stock" of one's life as being much like driving down the highway in your car. Up ahead, through the windshield, you see what's in store for you. Through the rearview mirror, you see what's behind you, or in your past. There you are, in the middle of this time continuum, in the driver's seat.

Finally, more and more people your age end up in the obituary column. Your doctor starts prefacing each answer to your health questions with "Well, for a person your age ..." You tell friends you've decided to go back to school, and to their horrified response, *"WHY ??!!"* tells you what they are really thinking ... (*Why study for all those tests, you'll be dead soon.*)

Take out a tape measure and expand it until it is 80 inches long (just like our 80 years of life expectancy. Now place your finger on the number that represents your current age. How many inches (years) are behind you, and how many years left? You have arrived at life's Twilight Zone ... the transcendence of self.

This transcendence of self leaves you wanting answers to the meaning of life, your life. You look to a higher power that can help make sense of your world, so you can feel that everything will be OK.

Discovering or creating the answer to life is transcendence, wisdom. You possess the faith that all is well, a higher power is watching over a pre-determined plan. There is strength in transcendence, a strength that guides us to healthier living that helps defy disease and conquer death.

WISDOM AND TRANSCENDENCE

Research confirms that the greater one's age, the greater their belief in God. A cross-national study by Professor George Bishop of the University of Cincinnati concludes that elders, boomers, and Gen-Xers believe human life began as the Bible says it began. *Praise the Lord, and Pass the Ammunition*, a World War II song, underscores the importance of covering all the bases, calling upon divine intervention as well as self-help.

The current demand for non-traditional sources (those previously ignored by science) for health maintenance and health care has created an entire industry of new-age treatments and supplements. There's been such a groundswell of alternative health publications, research, and lifestyle habits that the government established a new research institute to study the impact of non-traditional healthcare.

This new institute is housed within the National Institutes of Health and called the National Center for Complementary and Alternative Medicine (www.nccam.nih.gov).

IS HEALTH HEAVEN-SENT?

Where would modern healthcare be if it were not for its foundations in religious traditions and doctrines? The establishment of the first known hospital in ancient Turkey in 370 B.C. was in response to a Christian text: "Then the righteous will answer him and say, 'Lord, when did we see you hungry and feed you, or thirsty and give you drink? When did we see you a stranger and welcome you, or naked and clothe you? When did we see you ill or in prison, and visit you?' And the king will say to them in reply, 'Amen, I say to you, whatever you did to one of these least brothers of mine, you did for me'" (Matthew 25:37-40, New American Bible). In the early 1800s, Florence Nightingale, in response to a call from

God, established the care-giving tradition now known as Modern Nursing.
The establishment of the National Center for Complementary and Alternative Medicine confirms that many ancient traditions in healing merit a place of respect in modern medicine.

- The harmony of Buddhist Tradition gave rise to acupuncture as a method of achieving healthful balance in life.
- The Mormon Doctrine advocates a diet of vegetables, fruits, and whole grains, now embraced by USDA scientists.
- Jews and Muslims are spiritually directed to avoid certain meats, and modern science and today's health experts agree.

RELIGION VERSUS FAITH AND PRACTICE

The following studies underscore the role and value religion plays in health and longevity. It seems not to matter which religion one adopts, as long as you profess and practice that faith. Active participation in religion is the key.

- The University of Michigan studied the positive impact of *religious-based coping mechanisms* in reducing chronic pain and improving health status. Religious seniors were better able to cope with stressful living conditions found in poor neighborhoods.
- In a Kansas City study, Dr. Steven Lamm randomly assigned all new patients to one of two groups: those who received prayers and those who received the usual care. Those who received *prayers fared better* than those who did not.
- Duke University researcher Dr. Harold G. Koenig found that those who attended weekly religious service, prayed or studied the Bible daily had a 40 percent *lower rate of hypertension* than those who were less spiritually active.
- University of California-Berkeley scientists studied eight thousand men and women and found that *death rates were two to three times lower* for those who had social ties such as healthy relationships and deep spiritual beliefs.

- The Dartmouth Medical School found *a strong relationship between higher self-esteem*, less depression, and better physical health. Dartmouth scheduled 230 men and women for open-heart surgery. Six months after surgery, twenty-one people had died, but not one of those who professed deep religious beliefs was in this group.
- Pennsylvania State University and the University of North Carolina at Chapel Hill researchers discovered that religious seniors, those who attend or led services, taught Sunday school or attended religion classes, prayed, and listened to religious broadcasts *enjoyed better health* and greater happiness than those less spiritually active.
- Iowa State University studied religious observance and grandparent involvement with young children. Researchers found spiritually active elders enjoyed *more positive family relationships*, strengthening emotional and physical health.
- University of Michigan researchers found when religion is an important part of a mother's life, she's likely to feel she has a *better relationship with her adult children*, and her children are likely to report having a better relationship with her.
- Some doctors put religion on par with physical exercise because of *religiosity's tendency to reduce depression*, says the Human Population Lab in Berkeley, California. Religious involvement, say researchers, is an effective coping mechanism for elders undergoing stressful times.
- Dr. Christopher G. Ellison (University of Texas-Austin) and Dr. Jeffrey S. Levin (National Institute of Healthcare Research (NIHR) report that, "On average, high levels of religious involvement are moderately associated with better health status." The research team explored a range of explanations for the positive health effects of religious practices and spiritual beliefs, many have been *scientifically demonstrated to promote health and reduce disease*.
- University of Michigan researchers found the importance a mother places on *religion is a powerful predictor* of the quality of her emotional relationship with her child. Religious themes such as tolerance, patience, and unconditional love

strengthened relationships. There were no differences in the quality of mother-child relationships by religious affiliation; the study concluded that religious affiliation is secondary to the inner importance that one places on religion, for the quality of mother-child relationships.

THE SIX HEALTH BENEFITS OF FAITH

A common theme resonates among these studies. Spirituality in one's life, especially as you grow older, produces at least six benefits.

1. Healthy Behavior

Religious involvement may discourage behavior that increases health risks, such as tobacco and alcohol consumption, or it may encourage other positive lifestyle choices.

2. Social Support

People who regularly attend religious services appear to have larger and deeper social networks to provide emotional support and other forms of assistance than less-frequent attendees.

3. Self Esteem

Religious involvement may promote feelings of self-worth and confidence in the ability to control one's own affairs and destiny.

4. Coping Skills

Prayer, meditation, and other religious activities may help people deal with stressful events and conditions.

5. Positive Emotions

Religious activities lead to positive emotions influence immune functions and physiological factors that influence health.

6. Healthy Beliefs

Faith may provide a positive outlook that offers both emotional and tangible means of promoting individuals' health and well-being.

SCIENCE GETS A HEALTHY DOSE OF SPIRITUALITY

Today's patients believe their physical, mental, and spiritual health are interrelated (National Institute for Healthcare Research-NIHR). In response, the NIHR has funded curriculum development in medical schools in order to help new doctors become sensitive to their patients' spiritual side. The NIHR curriculum initiative teaches new doctors and medical faculty to achieve four goals.

GOAL ONE:
Learn about the overall knowledge, skills, and attitudes toward spirituality in the health care system.

GOAL TWO:
Apply spiritual knowledge to professional skills and attitudes in the care of their own patients.

GOAL THREE:
Learn how spirituality is involved in interactions between doctors and patients.

GOAL FOUR:
Learn how to teach about spirituality in clinical encounters.

Spiritual well-being is an important part of holistic medical care, say recipients of NIHR funding in support of the spiritual curriculum. *Spirituality and Medicine Curricular Awards* were sponsored by the John Templeton Foundation to recognize model programs in spirituality and health at medical schools nationwide.

The grants underscore the growing importance that medical schools are placing on responding sensitively to patients' spiritual needs. When the awards program began in 1995, only three of 125 medical schools offered courses on how to deal sensitively and effectively with patients' spiritual issues. Within a decade, half of all undergraduate medical schools were offering such courses.

A FINAL WORD

The roots of modern scientific medicine can be found in the ancient traditions and religious doctrines of Buddhism, Islam, Judaism, and Christianity. Medical research continues to confirm the validity and role spirituality plays in health maintenance and longevity.

ZOOMER-FRIENDLY READING – SPIRITUAL FITNESS

All Things Possible: Faith, Football, Miracle Season
Warner (2011).

The Purpose Driven Life: What Am I Here For?
Warren (2002).

Spiritual Literacy: Reading the Sacred in Everyday Life
Brussat and Brussat (1998).

Survival of the Religious
Helm et al. Journal of Gerontology: Medical Sciences (2000).

Creating a Spiritual Retirement
Srode (2003).

Power of Prayer
Salwak (1999).

If You Want to Walk on Water, Get Out of the Boat
Ortberg (2001).

Health Practices and Cancer Mortality among Mormons
Journal of the National Cancer Institute (1989).

Spirituality and Patient Care
Koenig (2002).

Realized Religion: Religion and Health
Chamberlain and Hall (2000).

God for the 21st Century
Stannard (2000).

Healed by Morning: Messages from God
Barrett (2002).

Religion in Aging and Health
Levin (1993).

Aging, Spirituality, and Religion
Kimble and McFadden (2003).

Awakening the Buddha Within
Surya Das (1998).

The Mormon Experience: A History of the Latter-Day Saints
Arrington and Bitton (1992).

Building Bridges: Christianity and Islam
Elias (1997).

Doorway Thoughts: Cross-Cultural Health Care
American Geriatrics Society (2004).

Fast Lane to Heaven: A Life After Death Journey
Dougherty (2002).

After Heaven: Spirituality in America Since the 1950s
Wuthnow (1998).

Experiencing the Soul: Birth, Life, After Death

Rosen and Burstyn (1998).

The Applause of Heaven
Lucado (1999).

When Bad Things Happen to Good People
Kushner (2001).

More Than Meets The Eye: Death, Dying, and Afterlife
Perry (2005).

The God Gene: How Faith Is Hardwired into Our Genes
Hamer (2005).

Spirituality and Aging
Atchley (2009).

10	# Retire Ready: Nothing To Do, All Day To Do It

Zoomers engage in early and sound retirement planning capable of supporting their anticipated standard of living.

R etirement is a health hazard! That's not an opinion. It's a fact. More than three decades ago, the American Medical Association proclaimed enforced idleness, like retirement, is a health hazard. Without proper retirement preparation, what you don't know can hurt you. In other words, "Ignorance smarts."

Retirement? Work, play, both? Time to get ready. Reminds me of that Paul Simon melody, *"Make a new plan, Stan. No need to be coy, Roy. Just set yourself free, Lee."* Today's economic environment has made it both fashionable and financially prudent to retire from one career to a second or third career. However, if you planned early and well, you may not have to work at all. But wealthy or not, a week full of Saturdays doesn't sound like an exciting way to spend the rest of your life.

YOUTH'N UP: RETIREMENT READINESS QUICK TIPS

➤ Since 1900, the average time-frame of retirement expanded a one-thousand percent, 6 months to 18 years (Demko, 2003).

➤ Life expectancy for white-collar males, age 65, is 36 to 40 months (NIMH).

➤ American workers continue to retire at an earlier age, 55 years old (NCHS).

➤ Retirees need 80% of work income to sustain lifestyle.

➤ 80% of all workers do not relocate after they retire.

➤ Couples should stagger their retirement dates by 6 months.

➤ 65 year olds can expect to live another eighteen years.

➤ 80% of elder care is provided by family, not government.

➤ AMA calls forced retirement a potential health hazard.

➤ Top five places to retire (Forbes, March 2011) are: Albuquerque (NM), Charleston (SC), Charlotte (NC), Colorado Springs (CO) and Fargo (ND). The last two cities must have been recommended by someone who never had to shovel through a snowdrift. No worries. By now, every new retiree has already relocated to these locations. So, keep an eye out for Forbes' next Retirement Location List.

RETIRING RETIREMENT

Whose idea was it that we retire in the first place? Before you start planning for your so-called retirement, better do a reality check then decide whether or not you should retire at all. Over the last 100 years, retirement has taken on many faces.

In 1937, the year the Social Security system started, the worker to pensioner ratio was thirty-two workers paying into the system for every one retiree drawing a pension. This ratio, now 3:1, will be

1:1 when the next generation retires. Today's 20 and 30 year olds will need to earn enough money to support themselves, their kids, aged parents, and one person who is getting a Social Security pension check.

Here's the best retirement advice you'll ever get: Don't do it. Forget retirement. There is no such thing. Retirement is just a convenient invention created years ago as an avenue to clear the work place for new blood. Over the years, entire industries became beneficiaries of this new concept called retirement. Ironically, it seems that the last person to benefit from retirement is the retiree.

In fact, even before the AMA proclamation, studies by the National Institute of Mental Health suggested that the transition to retirement was so stressful that the average life expectancy of a white-collar male at age sixty-five was only thirty-six to forty months.

Here's what makes retirement planning so difficult. The definition of retirement for one generation often contradicts with the definition assigned to the next generation. Read on and see how and why the meaning of retirement is in a constant state of flux.

1900. There was *no such thing as "retirement."* People worked until they died, were injured or became too frail to work. The desire to remain self-reliant was so valued that not working was unacceptable. Gerontologist, Dr. Robert Atchley called retirement the "portent of embarrassment."

1935. Retirement was defined as *a post-work reward* for a lifetime of labor. Older workers were expected to adopt a passive lifestyle of rest and relaxation.

1960. Retirement became known as *a time to "give back"* by transiting into voluntary service, an opportunity to retain youthful status, regardless of one's chronological age.

1980. Retirement *meant an "active lifestyle."* Options for retirees expanded beyond voluntary service to exploration of new roles: second careers, advocacy, dabbling in the performing arts, or going back to school.

2012. Retirement means *working full or part time* in order to supplement one's income, often due to inadequate financial planning, or a genuine desire to remain active and engaged in the world.

3 WORDS ABOUT RETIREMENT: PLAN, PLAN, PLAN

Enjoying an active and productive retirement won't just happen. Retirement is more a state of mind of life. Retirement is doing what you want to do, even if that choice is to continue to work. Keep the following realities in mind when planning for retirement.

Ask yourself why you want to retire.
Don't do it just because you hate the daily drill of your job. If you don't like your job, change your job.

Find out what makes you tick.
What makes your life inspiring, worth living? Did you ever wonder why many self-employed people never retire? Their retirement reward is to be able to continue to pursue their lifelong passion.

Force yourself to set lifestyle goals.
Since you can look forward to another two decades, plan to make it as interesting as possible. Make a list of ten things you would love to do if you could afford to retire. Then write down how much time you're spending in these activities right now. If these activities are not part of your current lifestyle, what makes you think your preferences will change in retirement?

Try to see through the dollar signs.
A common mistake is to focus strictly on the financial aspects of retirement. Everyone should have a retirement nest egg. But what's the point if you aren't healthy enough, or don't live long enough to enjoy the opportunities afforded to you by your retirement income?

Boomers are not ready for retirement.
The majority of boomers have done virtually nothing to prepare for retirement (News Max). Only 24% of boomers report being "very confident" about adequacy of retirement savings (TIAA-CREF).

Boomers will need to down-size their retirement dreams.
They won't be financially capable of retiring in the same style as their parents. That's the bad news. The good news is that the boomers will have to make their retirement decisions more carefully, and may decide not to retire at all. The Boomers will end up re-defining the meaning and purpose of retirement.

HOW TO MAKE RETIREMENT WORK

Those expecting a fulfilling retirement need to address the following considerations before they even think about retiring.
Here's the list.

Make two lists: *Your Life Now and Your Life in Retirement.* The first list details your typical twenty-four-hour pre-retirement day. The second list details your typical twenty-four-hour retirement day. What's different about the lists? What steps do you take to prepare for the differences? The typical retirement "honeymoon" lasts six to twelve months, sometimes less. Make sure to set new directions for the remainder of your retirement life, which is likely to be, at least, fifteen to twenty more years.

Health and Wellness: The key to good health is practicing prevention. This is a two-way street. First, work hard at staying fit; a nutritionally sound diet and exercise (cardiovascular and strength training) programs are a must. Second, monitor your unique health risks (those inherited from family genes, those unique to your age and gender, and those health risks unique to your ethnicity).

Relationships: Diversity is the Key. Make it a point of getting to know people of many interests, of many different ages, (younger, same age, and older than you). This support network of an intimate-significant other, an inner circle of close friends, companions who share experiences (travel, sporting events, shopping, entertainment), professionals who can address your needs (physician, accountant), email-only acquaintances, and pen pals can provide a variety of opportunities for socialization.

Housing and Location: If you plan to stay in your current home, as 80 percent of all retirees do, then take care of major repairs and remodeling before you start living on a fixed retirement income. Have a real estate attorney investigate reverse mortgage options that allows you to stay in your home while using the equity to finance necessary expenses like homecare or chore service. If you plan to relocate, learn about and visit age-integrated and age-segregated communities, rentals and purchase options, rental retirement communities, continued care retirement communities, life-care communities, assisted living (if needed now or in future), and shared housing.

Financial Planning: You will need money for ongoing expenses (power, light, water, cable TV, routine home maintenance); emergency situations (a six-month, immediately available cash reserve for health, family, and accidental crises); discretionary spending for personal enrichment such as entertainment, dining out, travel, anniversary and birthday gifts; and a hedge against inflation.

Sources of Income: At a minimum in today's present economy, you will need 80 percent of your working income, plus a hedge against inflation, in order to continue living at your current quality of life. The remaining 20 percent refers to expired expenses such as your home mortgage, college tuition, and car insurance for a teenage driver. Your retirement portfolio should include guaranteed income (such as pensions, money market CDs, bonds, social security) and growth opportunities for a hedge against inflation (such as real property, mutual funds, investment portfolio, antiquities, precious metals, or gemstones). Remember, your home does not represent available income unless you sell it, rent out space, acquire a reverse mortgage, or take in a working boarder in exchange for chore services (have your attorney create the lease agreement).

Transition to Retirement: When and where will all this retirement planning take place? Whatever your age, start planning now. After all, retirement planning is one segment of your overall life-work plan (education, career, marriage, family). If you plan to retire as a couple, then plan together. A national survey of pre-retirees found that two out of every five adult couples had never discussed when to retire, where to retire, or how much money they will need in retirement. Retire consecutively (taking turns, one first and the other within six months). Concurrent (both at the same time) retirement leaves neither spouse emotionally available to fully support the other.

REASONS NOT TO RELOCATE AT RETIREMENT

Those who plan to retire to their summer vacation home.
The two weeks you spend at the vacation home may bear no resemblance to the weather, activities, and opportunities available during the remaining fifty weeks.

Those who plan to retire to the same town as their adult children.
Sweet thought. Unfortunately, adult children relocate as many as five times during their career with the grandchildren in tow.

Those who plan to retire to their favorite resort town.
Quaint, relaxing resort towns have a way of attracting more people, more growth…increasing congestion, public facilities, cost of living, and taxes.

Those who plan to retire to any place that's warm.
Moving to a new location just because it's warm may not be a good decision if the lifestyle, health facilities, and cost of living are out of your league.

Those who dream of retiring to a golf or tennis community.
It's amazing how many people plan to golf every retirement day, but have never picked up a golf club. You might find the game boring, then what?

Informed decision-making helps ensure your new retirement plan fits like a glove. When it comes to eyeglasses, shoes or a retirement plan, one size does not fit all. The Relocation Readiness Quiz," (below) will help prepare you to make one of the many retirement decisions ahead.

Retirement Relocation Readiness Quiz (Demko, 2008)

Read each statement, determine how many apply to you, and then add up the points assigned to each of your selections. The higher your score, the more likely you are to relocate upon retirement.

- An empty nest will let me move on in my life. (+3)
- I am emotionally ready for the kids to leave home. (+1)
- The wanderlust of my youth is re-awakening in me. (+2)
- Life is more romantic now that "we're home alone." (+1)
- I plan to relocate once the kids are grown and gone. (+3)
- I plan to live in a community with people my own age. (+3)
- It's a possibility my adult kids will move back home. (+2)
- Adult kids who move back are obligated to pay rent. (+2)
- I expect to be debt free (mortgage, loans) when I retire. (+1)
- My income will increase when I am an empty-nester. (+2)

Retirement Relocation Readiness Quiz Key

If your score is: You should start to:
00 - 04 points   retro-fit home environment to evolving needs
05 - 07 points   learn retirement housing options and standards
08 - 10 points   tour communities that address your preferences

RELOCATION-READINESS RESOURCES

Here's your homework assignment (three resources: A, B, C, D) for settling the issue of retirement housing and location.

A. Learn Standards of Comparison

The Best Places to Retire (Forbes, 2011). An excellent resource for comparing retirement locations based on uniform, objective criteria. Once you decide on location, go to the next resource to learn about housing options.

B. Review Your Options

Visit the Senior Outlook Web site at www.senioroutlook.com, which will help you locate photographs of retirement communities in your geographical area. Remember, beauty is only skin-deep. Limit your housing options to facilities operated by management companies with an excellent track record.

C. Choose Your Options Wisely
Visit the AARP Web site at www.aarp.org/life/housingchoices. This site reviews the many types of retirement communities, explaining what could become an otherwise confusing array of housing options. You will also find help for evaluating your housing needs, and matching them to the appropriate type of housing option.

D. Choose Not to Choose
Not everyone relocates after retirement. In fact, the broad majority, 80 percent, do not relocate, preferring instead to remain in familiar territory surrounded by friends, family, and an established social network.

A FINAL WORD
I conclude this chapter with the immortal words of two personalities who, despite strikingly different lifestyles, share a common philosophy about life, and a penchant for using the word, "ain't."

"He who ain't busy being born is busy dying." (Songwriter, Bob Dillon). "It ain't over 'til it's over." (Baseball legend, Yogi Berra). So, ask yourself. "Am I a finished product, or a work in progress?

ZOOMER-FRIENDLY READING – RETIRE FIT
What Color is Your Parachute 2012: a practical manual for Job-Hunters and Career-Changers
Bolles (2011).

Spa and Resort Wellness Centers
www.traveltowellness.com

Retirement Without Borders
Golson and Golson (2008).

The New Retirement
Cullinane and Fitzgerald (2007)

When Death Occurs
Reigle (2003).

AARP: Retirement Housing Options
www.aarp.org/life/housingchoices

Retirement Preference Calculator
www.retiringbydesign.com

AARP Retirement Planning Calculator
www.aarp.org/work/retirement-planning/retirement_calculator/

Social Security Retirement Benefits Calculator
www.ssa.gov/planners/calculators.htm

The Original Death Calculator
www.AgeventureNewsService.com/deathcalculator.htm

11 Intellectual Fitness: Get Age-Smart

Zoomers know the difference between primary (inevitable) and secondary (reversible) aging.

There's good reason why Alcoholics Anonymous (AA) has the highest rate of success above all other recovery groups. AA's slogan acknowledges the importance of knowing what you can and cannot change about your life, and the wisdom to understand the difference. The same logic applies to human aging. Why you age is up to nature, but how you choose to age is up to you. *You may not be able to change your life, but you can change the way you live it.*

YOUTH'N UP: AGE-SMART QUESTIONS

➢ Can you list 5 losses and 5 gains associated with aging?
➢ Is achieving a great age a sign of strength or weakness?
➢ In years, give your biological, emotional and social ages?
➢ List, in rank-order, the body systems that age the fastest.
➢ Explain the difference between aging and chronic disease?
➢ How does the process of life-review cultivate wisdom?
➢ Who is more valuable to society, a 10, 40, or 80 year old?
➢ List key differences between gerontology and geriatrics.
➢ What number of years would you like to live, and why?
➢ How does increasing the length of life decrease its value?

DID YOU KNOW?

Life extension research is like a deck of cards scattered in fifty-two directions. The only way to make sense of it all is to gather up the cards and organize the deck. This chapter reviews major life-extension theories then organizes that knowledge into a nine-step plan for staying younger, longer.

There are geographical regions throughout the world where people incorporate life-enhancing habits into their daily routine. Life expectancy in Monaco, for example is 89 years. Other regions do not fare so well, such as Afghanistan where life expectancy only 42 years. Given economic differences between these regions, you might expect that wealth is a major factor in life expectancy. But, that's not true.

The USA spends more on health care per capita than any other nation in the world. Yet, USA life expectancy (80 years) ranks number 50 in the world. Forty-nine other nations have higher life expectancies than the USA even though Americans are well educated and affluent. Knowledge isn't power until you put that knowledge to good use. Most Americans know, but ignore, the fundamental rules for sustaining a long and healthy life.

Many so-called "inevitable" processes of aging are often reversible conditions. Diet, nutrition, meaningful life roles, exercise, spirituality, family ties, and environmental quality all vary widely throughout the world. These varied social-environments, therefore, result in varying life expectancies.

Secondary Aging and Primary Aging: the big difference

Secondary aging refers to all the changes that are associated with advancing age but not caused by the normal aging process. These changes are chronic diseases such as hypertension, cancer, and diabetes. These "problems" have known origins and respond to medical intervention, hence the name, secondary aging.

Primary aging refers to our "biological clocks." In this case, science understands how age-changes occur (chemical, hormonal, genetic) but does not know the origin of the changes. As a result, no treatment can be created. When the origin of an age-related condition is known, then treatments are created, and the conditions are no longer referred to as "primary aging" (changes of unknown origin) to "secondary aging" (treatable conditions that respond to medical intervention.

Life Span and Life Expectancy: the big difference

Life span refers to the maximum number of years it is possible for a human to live, which is 120 years. Life expectancy is the number of years one can "expect" to live, which is currently 80 years. Conquering secondary aging (chronic disease) raises life expectancy. Controlling the mechanisms of human aging (primary aging) results in raising our life span from 120 years to 800 years, or perhaps eliminating death altogether in a world where DNA mapping, genetic engineering, stem cell research, cryogenics and cloning provide mankind with perpetual rejuvenation. Yesterday's science fiction is tomorrow's brave new world.

Theories on Human Aging

Organizing the various theories on human aging begins with categorizing groups of theory that share common themes. I choose the following themes or categories: *Internal Variables*, *External Variables*, and *Moderating Lifestyle Variables*.

Category 1: Internal Variables (nature's programming)

This category of theories consist of all the variables each human being brings into the world—an inherited genetic code orchestrating the nature and scope of your human growth, development and risk factors based on family medical history.

Category 2: External Variables (nurture)

This category of theories consist environmental variables that carry the potential for altering our otherwise genetically-programmed process of human growth and development. Included here are factors related to both the *physical environment* (levels of toxins found in and around the home such as insecticides, cleansers and paint) and *social environment* (the quality of one's personal life and social network).

Category 3: The Moderating Variable: Lifestyle

This category of theories would consist of all the scientifically supported intervention strategies that promote "successful aging." These strategies (moderating variables) include health monitoring, health maintenance, and pro-longevity interventions supported by advances in cell biology, medical practice, assisted living devices, bionics, ergonomics, and wellness-lifestyle regimens.

CATEGORY I THEORIES: INTERNAL VARIABLES

Brain Rejuvenation

At birth, humans have ten billion brain cells (neurons). Once thought to be incapable of reproducing, new research confirms that neurons can and do reproduce. The Salk Institute, as reported by CBS News (*Adults Can Grow Brain Cells,* Dr. Emily Senay, 2009), found that the human brain has premature (undivided) neurons held in reserve, which are "somehow triggered to divide" in later life. It is yet uncertain how just how functional the cells are. In a related study (MIT News, 2012) researchers identified specific brain cells that activate only when learning occurs. These same cells were re-activated using opto-genetics (the use of light to re-activate specific brains cells which store memories). The re-activation allows the patient to recall a memory event in its entirety.

Biological Clock Theory (theory of planned obsolescence)

This DNA theory proposes an internally regulated "biological clock" first triggering growth, then deterioration, continuing decline, and ultimate death. Many theories on aging refer to Biological Clocks. Geneticists, for example, believe the body's circadian rhythms dominate all life functions; regulating sleep, hunger, and activity. Researchers at Colorado State University's Bioinformatics Center believe these biological rhythms have a 24-hour cycle that continually resets itself based on the rising and setting of the sun. Deprive a human being of their daily dose of sunshine results in sleeplessness, depression, and illness (AgeVenture, 2010).

Wear and Tear Theory (August Weismann)

This theory proposes the wearing out of both body systems and the cells that comprise those systems. The body's ability to "rejuvenate" itself by repairing injuries at the cellular, tissue, and system level suffers a slow, life-long decline which ultimately terminates life. Fixed commodities, essential to sustaining life, such as muscle mass, bone strength, body system integrity, capacity to repair and level of energy run down, run out and cause the body to simply stop working.

Cell Enzyme - Telomerase Theory (Geron Corp)

Telomerase is an enzyme that repairs and replaces telomeres, which are extensions of nucleic acids appearing at the ends of cell chromosomes. Each time a cell divides, the telomeres shorten. The integrity of the chromosomes is lost, resulting in cell damage and cell death.

Cell DNA Error Theory (Leonard Hayflick)

DNA errors result in the reproduction of increasing dysfunctional cells. As a result, the risk of "mortality doubles every seven years beyond the age of 30." (Hayflick, NEJM, 1976).

Free-Radical Theory (Denham Harman)

Cell damage can occur as a result of a molecule that has an "extra" electron, hence the name "free" radical molecule. This unbalanced molecule reacts destructively with normal molecules in the cell by "stealing" one of the normal molecule's electrons. The normal cell then becomes a free radical (due to its "stolen" electron). Cell structure is damaged to the extent that the by-product of cell digestion accumulates and the cell "drowns" in its own waste, unable to repair or reproduce itself.

Cross-Linkage Theory (Johan Bjorksten)

Loss of the skin's elasticity is the most apparent illustration of the devastating effects of cross-linkage. Collagen is a protein found in the skin, connective tissue, and bone. In youth, collagen is soft and flexible. Later in life, the collagen matrix cross-links, resulting in dehydrated, leathery, sagging skin. The cross-links slow down the delivery of nutrients into cells, and the export of wastes out of cells.

Pituitary Gland - Metabolic Theory (Donner Denckle)

Early in life, the pituitary sends messages throughout the body, stimulating growth, development and repair of injured tissue. In later life, this same gland may send a different signal. Harvard endocrinologist, Dr. Denckle proposed the existence of a Death Hormone released by the pituitary gland later in life that disrupts the cell's basal metabolic rate (BMR). BMR is the key process for transforming food into energy, which helps run the body. Disruption of the BMR results in cell death.

Thymus Gland - Immune Theory

The body's immune system is regulated by the thymus gland. As we age, we are more likely to become ill … and it takes us longer to recover from illness. That's because the thymus atrophies (shrinks) with age, from 225 grams at birth to only 3 grams at the traditional retirement age of sixty-five years. In extreme cases, the immune system loses its ability to distinguish between helpful and harmful elements.

As a result, the immune system attacks itself, leading to auto-immune diseases such as Type 2 (adult onset) diabetes and lupus.

CATEGORY 2 THEORIES: EXTERNAL VARIABLES

This category of theories refers to natural selection. Higher rates of survival are associated with your ability to adapt to two types of environments: the *bio-environment* and your *socio-environment*. Higher rates of survival (longer life) are associated how well your genetic makeup is compatible with the *bio-environment*, and how well you are valued by the people in your *socio-environment*. Incompatibility within one or both of these environments decreases your chances of remaining in the gene pool.

BIO-ENVIRONMENTAL THEORY

Exposure to toxins (food additives, air pollution, water pollution, household chemicals, or radiation) in our home, work, and public spaces accelerates the normal aging process. Exposure to excessive levels of otherwise "safe" chemicals, says the EPA, is associated with heart, lung, and liver disease, as well as, various types of cell cancers and DNA damage. Too much of a *good thing* can be a *bad thing*.

> ➢ BIO-ENVIRON - Homeostasis vs. Wear-Tear Theory
> Beginning at age thirty years, the efficiency of our body systems function at a reduced level, a one-percent decrease per year. For example, eighty-year-old kidneys filter toxins from the blood at a rate 50 percent less than that of a thirty-year-old. Our neurological, endocrine, and immune systems play a major role in healthy aging by supporting the body's adjustment to its environmental demands in response to regulation by our biological clock. This regulatory process is called homeostasis refers to the body's balance between external environmental demands and internal regulatory systems. The immune system helps control the extent to which environmental toxins succeed in influencing the normal functioning of the body's organ systems. Compromises in system function foster wear and tear.

➢ **BIO-ENVIRON - High Maintenance Homeostasis**
➢ This theory proposed by Carmelinda Ruggiero and Luigi Ferrucci revisits the *Rate of Living Theory* by focusing on homeostasis. Metabolism (the rate at which our bodies produce and burn-off energy during a resting state) is a key determinate of longevity. The lower the metabolic rate, the greater the potential for reaching maximum life span. This inherited factor offers a universal principle for explaining differences in longevity between individuals. For example, decreasing metabolic efficiency leads to dysfunction in our body systems, which in turn exhausts our energy reserve, which then results in increased frailty.

SOCIO-ENVIRONMENTAL THEORY

Your "place" in the world is negotiated between *your reality* (self-image) and *society's reality* (other people's perception of your worth and potential). The common theme among these theories is the goal of maintaining a sense of life-satisfaction. However, achievement of that goal has many different, and often opposing, strategies.

➢ **SOC-ENVIRON - Social Activity Theory**
➢ "Active Lifestyle" is the new retirement mantra. "I'm too darn busy to die." Stay active and you will stay happy. Taking on new roles and engaging in activities for activity-sake, is believed to support self-image and life-satisfaction. The absence of social activity leads to the individual's demise. Next time a grandma visits, assign her an activity that says, "Your participation is valued."
➢ **SOC-ENVIRON - Disengagement Theory**
➢ With age comes physiological decline (decreased energy, strength), cognitive deficit (memory, problem-solving), and social devaluation (obsolescence of skills, decline in status, role-less-ness). Elders disengage from the mainstream of life in order to save-face, avoid feelings of incompetency. Accepting the elder's withdrawal preserves life-satisfaction. Attempts to force participation creates unwanted stress.
➢ **SOC-ENVIRON - Continuity Theory**

> Life satisfaction is maintained by continuing lifelong roles, interests, and activities. The late-Maggie Kuhn, founder of the Grey Panthers, an elder-advocacy group, began her career during the infancy of America's labor movement, female worker rights. Much later in life, Maggie continued advocating for oppressed groups, this time America's older population.

> SOC-ENVIRON - Theory of Margin

> Life is a balancing act, proposed University of Michigan the late Dr. Howard McClusky, U-Michigan Professor Emeritus. The balance is between our liabilities and our assets. Life's challenges represent liabilities (burdens, responsibilities, age deficits). The liabilities component of this theory represents the "load" we are required to carry through life. Assets (good health, family ties, and social support network) represent "resources" for coping with life's "load." According to the Theory of Margin, your PERSONAL POWER is determined by the ratio of life's LOAD to life's RESOURCES. Life-satisfaction increases when we have adequate resources for coping with the burdens (load) of everyday life.

CATEGORY 3 MODERATING VARIABLE:
LIFESTYLE

Boomers aren't just seeking more negotiating power in order to better navigate through the game of life. Boomers are creating new rules for the game itself. New rules based on new perceptions of what it means to be mature, and what it means to retire. Retirement, the last third of life, is no longer a time for slowing down. Retirement has been "re-invented" as a time for new beginnings, an orchard of opportunities ripe for the picking. Let's explore some typical strategies for re-negotiating or modifying life's journey.

> Reduction Theory

> Based on the work of UCLA's the late Dr. Roy Walford, this theory proposes that the conveniences of modern society (more leisure time, passive lifestyles) combined with excesses (eating faster than we walk) have eroded our ability to live

longer. Walford advocated a diet high in nutrients and low in calories, resulting in gradual loss of weight, more compatible with our metabolic rate. Low-caloric intake, high nutrients and moderate use of vitamin-mineral supplements (if needed) enhance our health status and extend our lives.

➤ **Anti-aging Theory**
➤ This theory advocates adopting all strategies deemed necessary for stopping or reversing age-related decline. Strategies address every dimension of an anti-aging lifestyle: cosmetic surgery for a youthful appearance; supplements for diminishing risks to chronic diseases; hormones to rejuvenate the body's chemistry to youthful levels; pursuit of non-traditional roles and atypical activities such as mountain climbing or sky diving. Anti-agers are re-igniting their life at the very time age-peers are winding down.

➤ **Exchange Theory (Dowd and Dowd)**
➤ This theory explains how the value of an individual or social group changes in concert with innovation in technology. Due primarily to technological advances, the knowledge and skills of older adults become outdated. As a result, society de-values the potential of older people because older people represent tradition, the old ways of getting things done. Younger people, on the other hand, are more technologically literate. They are valued because their knowledge of, and skills in, advanced technology (e.g., computers, I-pods, cell phones) is up-to-date.

➤ **Youth'n® Theory (Demko)**
➤ This theory proposes that cultural habits and lifestyle choices undermine the process of successful aging. Over-eating, malnutrition, smoking, substance abuse, and lack of exercise are among the social factors which erode health status, and shorten life expectancy. Currently, 75 to 80 percent of all ailments and diseases affecting American adults are due to cultural factors, not the normal aging process. Address these lifestyle issues and life expectancy (now 80 years) will increase until it approximates human lifespan (120 years).

SUMMARY POINTS

- The process of human aging can be modified (slowed down).
- Science has identified life-extending modifications in aging.
- Inherited risks can be reduced by monitoring and treatment.
- Socio-environmental risks are reduced via a wellness lifestyle.
- Adding healthy, active years to life is now a viable option.

ZOOMER-FRIENDLY READING - AGE WISE

Use Your Brain to Change Your Age and look, think and feel younger every day.
Amen (2012).

Age Pages
National Institute on Aging, www.nia.gov

Key Indicators of Well-Being
www.agingstats.gov/agingstatsdotnet/Main_Site/Data/2010_
Documents/Docs/OA_2010.pdf

Medline: A-to-Z health reference
www.nih.gov

Adults Can Grow Brain Cells
CBS News, Dr. Emily Senay, 2009.
www.cbsnews.com/2100-204_162-21584.html

Brain Cell Breakthrough 2012
Researchers show that memories reside in specific brain cells
Cathryn Delude, Picower Institute for Learning and Memory, MIT News, 2012.

Constantly Curious: Stay Age Smart

A Zoomer cultivates a keen sense of intellectual curiosity, relying on trusted sources of longevity research.

E ach day, volumes of the latest aging research are heaped upon the summit of an already mountainous body of knowledge. Reports are filed, peer-reviewed for accuracy, then categorized to facilitate further research. Those who work in the field of aging often restrict their reading to their specialty in order to keep the task of literature review manageable.

Those working outside the field of aging might find the sheer volume of research literature mind-boggling unless it is organized into an understandable frame of reference. The process of categorizing all the literature on aging begins with organizing research findings first by discipline (i.e. gerontology, geriatrics, political, social, psychological, economic and so forth). Second, each discipline is then categorized by sub-topics (social: social work, demographics, social problems, and so forth). The third process involves further categorization according to the type of research methodology used to create the new knowledge. While the first two processes are self-explanatory, the third categorization process (research methodology) is lesser known or understood by readers.

Qualitative and Quantitative Research

The body of knowledge in any field is generated from two different research methodologies: *qualitative* and *quantitative*. Qualitative research methodology focuses on creating new theory (logical explanation of a process such as describing the progressive stages of Alzheimer's disease, or the five stages of the process of dying, as proposed by Dr. Elizabeth Kubler-Ross). Once the theory is created, it must be tested for accuracy (validity) using a methodology called quantitative research.

Readers of qualitative (theory-producing) studies find that the author relies primarily on a narrative (words) defense of her theory. On the other hand, readers of quantitative (theory-testing) studies find that the author relies on a statistical (probability) defense of her findings regarding the theory's accuracy. The result is constant updating of the body of knowledge in a given field of study, in this case, knowledge about human aging.

Before moving on, it's important to note that both qualitative and quantitative research methodologies are sub-categorized by research design (the method by which data is collected and analyzed). Those interested in learning more should consult texts explaining the foundations of each methodology. Qualitative research methodology includes historical review, content analysis, and ethnographic methods for collecting and analyzing data. Quantitative research methodology includes survey research, experimental, cross-sectional studies and longitudinal designs.

What follows is an annotated list of selected sources of knowledge created by both qualitative and quantitative research literature. These sources can be found in print and/or electronic format in most colleges and universities. If one of the sources ceases to publish, the archived issues may still be valuable. Check with your librarian for assistance.

Abstracts in Social Gerontology
Summaries of recent literature, cross-indexed from books, journals, and government publications in the social aspect of aging studies.

Activities, Adaptation and Aging
A peer-reviewed journal reporting both qualitative and quantitative research on the therapeutic value of activities upon the quality of life.

Ageing and Society
A journal of articles drawn from primary sources (reported in the researcher's own words) and secondary sources (reported by an editor).

Ageing International
Dedicated to the well-being of older persons worldwide; primary focus is on social and economic issues, public policies, and use of resources.

Aging and Mental Health
A journal reporting on normal and abnormal aging, psychological and psychiatric problems in later life, and therapy intervention strategies.

AgeStats.gov
An Internet site offering publications and statistical charts on various demographic and health characteristics of the elderly.

American Public Health Association at: www.APHA.org
See "Essential Public Health Services"

Biogerontology
A peer-reviewed journal devoted to modifying the aging process and developing theoretical models linking aging, survival, and healthcare.

Gerontechnology
Dedicated to designing technology and environments for safe, independent living and social participation of older persons.

Gerontologist
Focus of the journal is primarily in the area of social gerontology; articles are interdisciplinary in nature.

International Journal of Geriatric Psychiatry
Reports results of original research on the causes, treatment, and care of all forms of mental disorders that affect the elderly from a global view.

Journal of Adult Development
Focus is on positive aspects of adult development, cognition, developmental theories, and methodologies across the life span.

Journal of Aging and Social Policy
Analyzes policy-making as applied to health care, long-term care programs, income security, end-of life issues, and social welfare.

Journal of Cross-Cultural Gerontology
A forum for information on the aging process and problems dealing with non-western populations.

Omega
A major source concerned with aging and death with articles focusing on dying, death, bereavement, and suicide.

Topics in Geriatric Rehabilitation
A peer-reviewed health care publication focusing on the clinical and treatment aspects of geriatric care.

Your search for knowledge about aging and retirement is yours for the taking. Here are six ways to begin your search for information.

1. The library reference desk can help locate in-house and on-line resources, many of which are free or inexpensive.

2. Professional associations offer scientific journals and newsletters with valuable information posted on their web sites.

3. Public relations departments within research universities post press releases reporting the results of studies conducted by the faculty.

4. Try going on-line to your favorite web site search engine, type the key words associated with your question, and away you go.

5. Be sure your sources of information are based on reports in peer-reviewed (trustworthiness of the findings) journals.

YOUR NEW BEGINNING: Youth'n Up, Get AgeVenturous

Time to "get pumped" about your potential and the opportunities that await those who still believe they are not a finished product, but *a work in progress, a masterpiece in the making.* Use your new knowledge to *Youth'n Up* your life and start living the ZOOMER lifestyle, today! *Stop acting your age, start living your life.*

About the Author

Dr. Demko is a University of Michigan doctoral graduate with certifications in gerontology (University of Michigan), geriatric functional assessment (USF-Medical), retirement planning (AARP) and a certified Master Teacher (NCSPOD).

Challenges to our traditional notions about aging and retirement are published under the author's trademark works: *OPALS* (Older People with Active Lifestyles), *AgeVenture* news magazine, and *ZOOMER* lifestyle magazine.

In broadcast media, the author's work appeared on NBC Today, Fox & Friends, CBS, National Public Radio, Clear Channel TV, Fox Radio, Sony TV's Life & Style, London's BBC and talk-radio in USA, Canada, England, Ireland, New Zealand and Australia.

In print media, the author's work is quoted in *Glamour*, *Readers Digest*, *New York Times*, *New York Post*, *Los Angeles Times*, *Atlanta Constitution*, *Maxim*, *Marie Claire*, and *Forbes*.

Praise for Professor Demko's gerontological work includes:

- *"we loved your interviews"* London BBC Live Radio
- *"a new attitude about age"* New York Times
- *"the age guru, Dr. Demko"* Maxim magazine
- *"the A-list of sources on age"* Palm Beach Post
- *"One of our favorite guests."* SONY Life & Style Television
- *"Dr. Demko coins ZOOMER"* AARP Global Network
- *"Demko's ZOOMERS are boomers with zip!"* Forbes.

Contact Information:
www.demko.com
demko@demko.com
demko@umich.edu
561-866-8251
904-629-6020

www.ingramcontent.com/pod-product-compliance
Lightning Source LLC
Chambersburg PA
CBHW020437290526
45785CB00002B/896